A Mindful Appro~
Ownershi

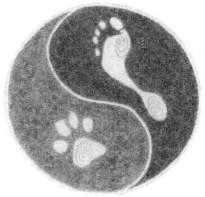

www.mindfulmutts.co.uk

Original artwork by David Shepherd

Artache

Contents

Introduction

Developing and maintaining a balanced relationship with your dog is an ongoing process and will continue to evolve as your understanding of each other grows. The ideas presented here will hopefully become part of your routine and eventually second nature. You will be able to communicate more effectively with your dog, leading to a happier life together. Dogs need leadership and we need to lead; this is a necessary part of creating and maintaining a close bond and loving relationship with our pet dogs. Our philosophy focuses on **state of mind, energy and fulfilment** and the effects these have on how we interact with our dogs, and on how they respond to us.

Why this book?

This book will take you on a journey of discovery into Mindfulness and how being Mindful can benefit you and your dogs. It has been inspired by our 'Beyond Obedience' classes and expanded from the course notes and handouts.

You might be wondering what Mindfulness has to do with dogs. This is how we made the connection…

…When we were having problems with our own dogs, the behaviourist we worked with explained how our energy was affecting our dogs and how we needed to calm down and be more balanced. What he didn't actually explain was how to recognise when we were not calm and balanced, or, how to become calm and balanced. And what *was* this energy thing he kept talking about? We spent a couple of years going on weekly pack walks with up to twenty other dogs with 'issues'. We learned so much about how dogs communicate with each other and started to recognise the difference in the mood and energy of the people and their dogs. With all of the talk about awareness of our own energy and the responsibility we have for our dogs, we were drawn to, and attended some Mindfulness classes. During one of these classes the instructor described, what to us, was the same as what the behaviourist had said about the psychology of our dogs, and the penny finally dropped; dogs live mindfully. It's all about the moment for them. Understanding this helps us to see the world from their perspective. Mindfulness became our way of being and as a result we are both calmer and happier people. We soon realised that Mindfulness was the perfect way of explaining how to recognise what is going on in terms of our thoughts, feelings, emotions and generally, what we are sharing with our dogs. Our ongoing studies and passion resulted in us becoming qualified dog behaviourists and Mindfulness Practitioners with a mission to help everyone discover their inner dog. Our approach is more biased to the psychological, mental and spiritual aspect of creating or bringing a dog back into balance. A balanced dog should be able to have an appropriate emotional response to the events of daily life. They should be able to control their emotions and not be over-stimulated or over-excited by other exciting events around them. They will have a confident, relaxed energy that will diffuse tension when meeting other dogs singularly or in groups.

In order to help our dogs be balanced it helps if we are too. We need to be able to lead them with a balanced, confident energy for them to be able to feel safe. If we can't control our emotions, if we get angry and frustrated, or lose our tempers and shout at them, we lose their trust. They just take it that if you can't control yourself, why should I follow you? how are you going to keep me safe? So the focus is on us to give them time, space and to create the right environment for our dogs to thrive. This is a training manual for you, the guardian, not a training guide for dogs.

We have kept this book short and to the point. The aim is to simplify the way we train, work and ultimately live with our dogs. We have kept it simple because, really, it is. The pet dog 'industry' has artificially complicated things almost beyond comprehension. Choosing to focus on selling tools to mitigate certain behaviours, such as a harness to stop a dog pulling, originally designed to enable dogs to pull weight comfortably. Or an extendable lead for the dog that won't come back when let off lead, so the dog never has to learn to follow their owner or come back when called, or experience true freedom (not perceived). People buy into the effective marketing around these tools as they look like the perfect solution, and are always portrayed as the kind thing to do for your dog, but they are simply treating the symptom rather than the problem. Time then, to go back to the basics of how to set yourself and your dog up for a happy peaceful life together. This is the foundation of making sure your dog can cope with the calamity of everyday human life and activities.

We start with an introduction to Mindfulness which we hope will pique your interest enough to continue to find out more and adopt it as a way of life. Then we look at how this applies to working with your dog's energy and state of mind including some basic body language signals to help understand their state of mind in that moment. We have included some basic exercises that will help with your dog's self control and confidence and some Mindfulness exercises for you.

How to get the best out of this book

To get the most out of this book we would recommend going through it in order, as each chapter builds on the last, furthering your knowledge and experience in a logical and organised way. It will also be useful to go back over earlier material to refresh your memory and practice. This is not a quick fix book as it may require a change in mindset or even lifestyle. As you will discover, if you keep going over the material it will soon become a part of your routine and then become second nature. Changing habits can be hard but you can be sure your dog will appreciate the effort.

Take your time with the exercises and meditations we have suggested for you, as it can feel a little strange if you have never done anything like this before. If you are patient with yourself and practice regularly you will find you start looking forward to, and, enjoying the space and peace they bring in a mad world.

The exercises we have included are to encourage both you, and your dog, to develop a sense of self awareness, self control and the ability to relax. When working with your dog, you are also having to work on yourself in order to bring the right energy to the session. This is where the power of Mindfulness really kicks in. It helps to bring ourselves into the moment (where our dogs are waiting for us). With a couple of deep breaths and asking what am I thinking? Feeling? What is happening in the environment around me? And how do I feel about it? So it may seem that you are just working with your dog, but you are actually having a very Mindful experience as there can be a lot going on under the surface.

We have assumed no level of knowledge or training. If you find some of the exercises are too easy for you or your dog, try to find ways to take it to the next level. The methods we have included are one way among many to accomplish the same results. If you have your own way that works for you, that's ok. For example, people often say of their dog "Oh, she can do down ok", but we ask can she do a twenty minute 'down-stay' in the park, at a distance, with other dogs running around? That's an extreme example and the answer is usually no, but it demonstrates that there are always new ways to challenge yourself and your dog.

The exercises for the dogs we have included – watch me, down, wait, go to place and leave – are foundational to the more complex behaviours we want from our dogs. For example, for your dog to wait patiently while you are preparing their dinner (or not get under your feet while you prepare yours) it would be ideal if they are able to go to place, down and wait. Then you can use 'watch me' to release them from this position. You will soon see how these transfer into other areas of your life, such as leaving the house, getting in and out of the car or going to the pub. And it all starts with you.

How It Began

The following stories briefly outline how all this started for us.

Jackie and Buddy

 It was 4pm on a Saturday and we were preparing to close the animal charity for the weekend, when we received a call about two puppies found tied to a tree in a local park. A kind lady had taken them in but couldn't keep

them herself. So the mission was on to find emergency foster accommodation at the weekend (always a tough call) None could be found so my colleague and I agreed to take one each over the weekend. We went to pick them up and were greeted by two beautiful Shepherd/Rottweiler mix boys. Needless to say during that weekend it became obvious that Buddy was staying with me and so our journey began.

Buddy was an amazing pup, he learned quickly and training him was a delight; he was a calm and very friendly boy. I have had dogs most of my life, the first being when I was 16. I have always enjoyed training and seemed to have a knack for it. All of my dogs have been extremely well behaved. Knowing Buddy was going to be a big dog I was extra vigilant with his training as I am a woman of 124lbs & he eventually grew up to be 110lbs. Buddy didn't let me down as he was a fabulous dog, extremely happy, obedient and super friendly with people and other animals.

Until, one fateful day when he was 18 months old. We were walking in the woods as we did most days, when Buddy suddenly ran over to a young dog and pinned it to the ground. I was in complete shock as he'd never done anything like that before. There was no biting or aggression, just pinning. I apologised profusely and moved on, we continued our walk with no further incidents. In the next few days we were in a different park and he did the same thing again. I was mortified and had no clue what was going on with him as nothing had changed; he was exactly the same, well behaved, friendly boy. The worst incident, which happened on the street brought the police to my door. We were walking along the street and I stepped to the side to let a man and his dog pass. Suddenly, unexpectedly and completely out of character Buddy lunged, the lead came out of my hand and he pinned the dog down and would not let it up. The man was screaming at me, I was screaming at Buddy, the man was threatening me with violence (not sure how that would have helped) and all I could do was to keep saying I'm sorry while trying to get Buddy off his dog. I walked away confused, upset and clueless as what to do. A few days later, a lone Policeman visited me. We weren't hard to find, everyone knew the woman with the big bear-like dog. He admitted to me that it was a call he had felt apprehensive about but on meeting Buddy he completely relaxed and agreed that Buddy was a calm, well behaved dog and could see no problem with him at all. As we talked I explained that I did not understand what was going on with Buddy so didn't know what to do about it and asked him where I could find advice but sadly he had no idea other that the obvious 'Google it' (which had yielded nothing) On leaving, he did say that if there was another complaint the situation could be very different.

That was the day that our lives changed drastically as I did the only thing I could think to do, and that was to avoid other dogs at all costs. This broke my heart and our old routine of going to the woods/park and Buddy playing and running with the other dogs became Buddy on lead walking the streets at times where there were likely to be fewer dog walkers. I was terrified the whole time and when I did see a dog my anxiety went through the roof. I suffered a lot of verbal abuse from people due to Buddy barking and lunging at almost all dogs by now. This really saddened me because I was asking for help but finding none and I just didn't know what was going on or what to do about it. It had become so distressing for me that even just thinking about going for a walk would have me feeling beyond anxious and this continued and heightened for the whole time we were out. I felt that I was letting Buddy down and that he no longer had a full life, I questioned whether I was the right person for him. Would he be better with someone else? What can I do? These are the thoughts I went to sleep with each night. I scoured the internet but could only find offers of training which Buddy did not need. This continued to be our life outdoors for a very difficult three years.

Then I heard about a man that met up our local woods at the weekend who helped 'problem dogs' I can't express the relief I felt (although still found myself thinking he may not be able to help Buddy). I literally went back to counting the number of sleeps until the Saturday meet up. When the day came I got Buddy in the car, went to the woods and headed for the meeting place (terrified I'd see a dog on the way) As we approached, Gabriel (the dog psychologist who ran the walks) told me to wait and he approached with his dog (a malamute). As soon as his dog was within striking distance Buddy pounced and pinned his dog to the ground I was mortified and half expected to be sent packing with my mad, bad dog. What I didn't expect was Gabriel just getting hold of Buddy, throwing him off his dog and basically daring him to do it again He didn't! Gabriel explained to me what was going on for Buddy, what he was doing and why he was doing it BUT the biggest kicker was when he explained to me how my energy and expectations of Buddy have a huge influence on how he interprets the environment and how he reacts to what he interprets. This is where I learned that training and behaviour (aka psychology) are two very different things.

These weekend walks became the highlight of my week. Buddy started off wearing a muzzle (along with a lot of the other dogs) which I hated at first, although it didn't bother him at all. This gave him the chance to spend three hours running, walking and relaxing with other (problem) dogs. Also allowing him to make the mistakes (with no risk to any dog), giving us the chance to correct it and show him another way. Buddy and I walked every Saturday and Sunday, and some weekends he would have no muzzle, depending on the other dogs in the pack that week. In the whole two years of doing these walks I didn't see one dog fail to thrive regardless of their original 'issues'. It was such a natural environment for the dogs and I was fascinated watching them interact with each other, the changing dynamics, especially when a new dog joined in. I saw dogs start the walk as mortal enemies only to become the best of friends by the end of the day. I learned so much and it awakened in me a real desire to better understand dogs, their motivations, their communication both with other dogs and us with two legs. Although the pack walks were completely safe and nobody was going to abuse me for anything Buddy might do, I still struggled to 'really' relax. I'd think I was doing great until I saw Buddy ahead either acting up or looking like he may be about to (which 9 times out of 10 never happened). Then all of those ingrained feelings, thoughts and reactions would be there and as much as I tried to change, it had become my normal over the three years. Those walks gave me so much and this is where I met Steve who was also there every weekend. We soon discovered that we were walking the same path both physically and metaphorically.

Steve and Kai

 This is supposed to be my life as a game developer and 3D animator. In the decade leading up to this point I had been a stay at home dad, played in three bands and done quite a lot of training for the future career when child duties lessened as they started big school and were more independent. During this time I had began to feel a bit isolated. There are lots of Mother and baby groups but not much choice for us dads and some days I would be the only person I spoke to. This sense of

isolation was compounded when I started working from home on my own, combined with feeling a bit redundant in the dad department as life was moving on and roles were changing. I had also recently given up smoking and was now sat in front of the computer with a plate of biscuits for hours a day and was piling on the pounds. In a fit of madness the solution came to me. Get a dog! We'd always wanted a dog but were unable to have one due to work and commitments, small child and holidays, but now the time was perfect. I was at home all day, it'd get me out for some exercise and I might even meet some people. What could go wrong?

So off to the shelter we went, which is where we met Kai, barking her head off, trying to squeeze herself through the bars. She was so excited by attention from us but she did a play-bow to us, which was a lot more interaction than we'd got from the other dogs there. She'd just been spayed and still had her cone on. This was battered, ripped and chewed to bits. They'd attached it with two collars and three boot laces in an attempt to stop her taking it off. Maybe that should have been a clue as to what we were in for.

Little did I know then that my life was about to change completely. The first walk was a complete shock. Kai is through the door like a rocket, with a hapless human stumbling after. She's  off up the road, flat to floor, literally pushing off with both back legs, bunny hopping. Obviously choking herself blue on the collar as all we had from the rescue was a collar and lead. After been dragged to the park, just about managing to hang onto her, Kai sees her first dog in the distance. At this point she quite literally turned into the devil. I'd only ever seen dogs like that in horror movies. I'd never been so shocked, bewildered or deflated as I felt that day. Speaking to the shelter about it, they told me that if she was returned she would be put to sleep because she was already on her last chance. Probably it would have been good to have been told this at the start of the process. I wasn't about to let her be put down though, so agreed to give it more time and get some training to sort her out. How hard could that be?

The local training class was full for the following three terms, nine months, but mentioned a class that was about fifteen miles away that had some spaces, so we put ourselves on the waiting list and got Kai booked in. That was when we discovered that Kai was not a good traveller. The inside of the car looked like a scene from the exorcist by the time we got to the first session. Then imagine taking the devil dog into a room full of other dogs. The first few weeks were spent sitting at the side just holding on to her. After a couple of months and a lot of car valeting she was able to participate more and did actually learn a couple of things.

Walks were still a nightmare. The pulling was really hard and relentless. It was a cold winter with lots of ice and snow and we all got pulled over several times. This would ramp up if we spotted another dog on the walk and it was almost impossible to hang on to her. My back was wrecked by this point.

The local training class became free and we were accepted. It was smaller class sizes and short sessions so with an inordinate amount of ham and cheese to keep her distracted she actually made a bit of improvement. To be fair she was actually doing great with her obedience stuff, I was doing a lot of training at home and she was a keen and able student. The next defining moment came during her exam for the Bronze Award. On the Stay test, where the owners had to be at least a metre away from the dogs, she seized her opportunity to attack the young Australian Shepherd that had been giving her the eye for the whole course. She failed her Bronze Award. I was kept back after class and lectured about what a dangerous dog I'd got, and how she'd never be able to be around other dogs and the best option would be to take her back. I explained that this would result in her being put down and the trainer agreed that might be the best option as she would never have a proper life. While I was being lectured Kai was just sitting there like butter wouldn't melt. I looked at her and the thought "You're just an aggressive dog sitting down" went through my head. This was the point I realised there is a vast difference between 'training' and 'behaviour'. All the advice I had found up until this point had been about positive only training and that teaching her to sit would somehow make her ok with other dogs. This was clearly not the case. We weren't invited back to do the Silver. Kai was still highly reactive to other dogs.

To call this a low point would be an understatement. Then I met Gabriel, a local dog behaviourist and started going on his weekend pack walks, where over the next three years I learned that Kai's behaviour was as much to do with me than it was her. I met Jackie and Buddy on these walks. We started walking together for moral support and as our friendship developed so did our passion for dogs and dog behaviour which eventually led to Mindful Mutts.

It's been an incredible journey of self discovery and learning. The journey to being qualified as a behaviourist and discovering Mindfulness has completely changed my life for the richer. I've gone from feeling like I was the only one, with no help that I could find, through all the mistakes and the failures, the crying and the soul searching, but more importantly, the successes, the people I met and the friends I made because our dogs had a fight. Hopefully now, my knowledge and experience can give others the help they need and the hope to pursue it.

So big breath, RELAX. And Let's go.

Chapter 1

What is Mindfulness?

In essence, Mindfulness as a concept is quite simple. Putting it into words however, is not. John Kabat Zinn, is accredited with introducing Mindfulness to the west, and coined the term Mindfulness. He explains it in the following quote:-

"Mindfulness is paying attention in a particular way; in the present moment, non-judgementally." - *John Kabat Zinn*

You might well say "Whaat?" In terms of a practical definition, Mindfulness is simply being in the habit of noticing your thoughts and feelings, thereby giving you the opportunity to choose how to think, feel and act in any particular moment.

Mindfulness as a concept comes from 2500 year old Buddhist teachings and science has eventually caught up. In Chinese, the word for Heart and Mind is the same. In the context of the language and culture it came from, it's meaning was more 'Heartfulness'. This was considered a bit too touchy feely for Western sensibilities, as we tend to prefer a mind focused intellectual approach to things, hence the term 'Mind'fulness. There are now thousands of scientific studies and trials proving without doubt that practising Mindfulness helps people to live a calmer, more balanced life.

The aim is to BE Mindful, not to DO Mindfulness. However, we have to DO mindfulness to begin with until habit starts to take over. In this book you will find examples of both 'formal' practices which involve meditations, and 'real world' Mindfulness, which help us navigate calmly through the twists and turns of the day. Consider the formal as going to the gym for your mind. This starts to build the strength and technique needed for use in everyday life.

The hardest part of Mindfulness is remembering to be Mindful. Using cues to remind you can be helpful, such as every time you go through a door, go up and down stairs, or when your mobile pings. You could set a phone alarm to go off every couple of hours or randomly, anything that will remind you to just take a few seconds to check in with yourself. This helps to develop the habit of Mindfulness.

What is mindfulness meditation?

Meditation is a word that conjures all kinds of images, thoughts and opinions, a lot of which are quite common, like it is necessary to sit cross legged for hours, or you need to be able to empty your mind of all thoughts. Various methods of meditation have been used as a way of escaping emotions and transcending states of consciousness. Mindfulness meditation on the other hand is the practice of focusing our awareness on the present moment by connecting with one or more of the five senses; sight, sound, touch, taste and smell or by simply observing the breath. Rather than trying to escape from feelings and thoughts, we acknowledge them and let them go. Zoning in, not zoning out. It has been shown that fifteen minutes of Mindful meditation a day can be of great benefit, so it doesn't have to take up a lot of time. Do you need to meditate to be mindful? The answer is no, but the practice does enhance your ability to focus your awareness on the present moment in your day to day life. It's like a musician practising scales and arpeggios. It gives them the strength and the dexterity they need when playing for real. At the very least, learning some kind of relaxation technique will be useful to help bring your breathing and any anxiety under control.

Meditation keeps you young

There is an element of truth to this and it's down to your telomeres. Telomeres are proteins located at the ends of chromosomes which protect the chromosomes during cell division. Telomeres degrade with each cell division and when they become too short or tatty, cell division can no longer take place. This is the cause of ageing. It has been shown that experienced meditators have longer, healthier Telomeres than non-meditators, therefore potentially living longer and ageing better. Studies have shown improvements in telomere health even after eight weeks of consistent meditation.

How does it help us?

Meditation causes physical changes to the brain. Recent advances in fMRI brain scanning have shown that just eight weeks of regular meditation makes measurable changes in the brain. Meditation actually increases the size of, and strengthens the grey matter of the frontal lobes. This leads to us being more focused, having a greater attention span, better problem solving abilities and also improves memory and learning. It has also been shown that activation of the brain's frontal lobes is proportional to activity in the limbic system, which is responsible for our emotional life. So if the frontal lobes have a lot of activity, the limbic system has less, and we become less emotionally reactive and less likely to over-react, in thoughts or actions. These changes in the brain are because of something called neuroplasticity which basically means that the more the brain practices an action or a thought the stronger the neural pathways involved become, these pathways are what determine our thoughts, feelings and actions. The more we repeat our 'usual' repertoire the more they become our 'normal' 'this is just how I am' etc. The more we practice being peaceful and balanced the stronger the pathways for that behaviour become and the more peaceful and balanced we become as a default way of being.

Real world Mindfulness

There are many ways to experience a mindful moment throughout the day. Bringing our full attention to everyday tasks such as peeling potatoes, washing up, having a shower etc. helps us to be in the present moment. We can scan through our senses for this. What can I feel? What can I hear? What can I smell? When eating or drinking, make the first bite or sip as mindful as possible by really noticing the smell, taste and texture. At first you will find your mind starting to wander onto different things. This is absolutely normal. When you notice you have drifted off, gently bring your attention back to what you are doing. It is this moment of noticing that your mind is somewhere else that is the essence of Mindfulness. You are not doing it wrong. Be kind to yourself, don't beat yourself up. In fact, the more your mind wanders the more practice you get. Practising in this way helps train your mind to focus and improves attention and concentration. When we are focused on the present moment we tend to let go of past concerns and future worries enabling us to be fully engaged with our everyday lives. We find we seek less drama, we are less quick to respond negatively in the moment and become generally less stressed.

The Pause

A good example of real world mindfulness is what we call 'The Pause'. This is good to use when going from one activity to another. Examples would be to do it at the start and end of your work day to delineate between home and work life. If you walk your dog to the park, use it to transition from the street walk to the park walk. You may not have noticed there's a little knot of anxiety, or you may have been rushing and would carry that into the park instead of a more relaxed walk. All it involves is stopping and connecting with the breath, and so the moment, for a couple of breaths. You can connect to any of the five senses or whip through them all, the point is to give 'a pause' between activities or changing situations.

How does it help our dogs?

Before we decide to get a dog we all have an idea or a vision of what having a dog will be like, such as running on the beach, long country walks, cosying up by the fire. Often this turns out to be very different to the reality; the dog chases everything, won't stop barking, won't come back when let off the lead and chews the furniture. It is this difference between the vision and the reality that causes us to look on the dog as having a 'problem' and how large we judge that 'problem' to be.

Your dog is already here in the moment, it's where they live ALL of the time; they are entirely present. They do not hold on to past events the way we do and they have no concept of the future. Dogs are very sensitive to our energy and moods and this can be very confusing for them, as we often say one thing but our energy is saying something different.

A common example of this would be that a person walking their dog is accosted by an over-excited dog of a particular breed and the interaction turns to growling and snapping or even a bit of a squabble. The owner is understandably shaken, a bit upset, maybe even angry. The next time they see a dog of that breed, the person tenses up, starts feeling anxious, puts tension on the lead and drags their dog away, whilst trying to reassure the dog that there is no problem. Their dog picks up on this change in energy, and the tension on the lead affirms to them that something is wrong. The dog will look for the cause and, noticing the other dog, put the blame there. They may even bark or lunge at the other dog to tell them to go away as they are upsetting their owner. This then proves to the owner that their dog doesn't like that particular breed and more or less guarantees this behaviour will happen every time they see one.

As our thoughts create our feelings and affect our emotions it makes sense that by being in control of what we are thinking we can also be in control of the way we feel. Think of something that angers you and you will inevitably start to feel angry, think of happy times and you feel the warm glow of those memories. Choose happy thoughts, why not?

When we are mindful we can let go of our frustrations and tension which means we interact with our dogs in a calmer more compassionate way. To enable our dogs to be in a calm, relaxed state of mind, we have to be in a calm, relaxed state of mind first. We can't be mindful with our dogs until we can be mindful with ourselves.

So using Mindfulness we can learn to be accepting of where we are on our journey with our dogs. Keeping your vision of the ideal life with your dog, is a great thing to do, but it is important to be focused in the present. This enables us to put past behaviour or events behind us and not use them as a way to predict future events. Watch out for the narrative running in your head like imagining the worst case scenario, or, this is what happened last time! etc. These inevitable stories, which we usually fail to notice, will lead to us thinking, feeling and acting in the same way.

A good way to start the process is to just notice how you feel, but in a non-judgemental way. Don't try to change anything or even question why you are feeling it at that moment. If you identify the feeling it can be useful to give it a label, "Oh that's frustration" or "That's anxiety". This not only diminishes its intensity but can also help us to recognise it at another time; however do not dwell on it, just move on.

It is important to be able to recognise these feelings and to accept them for what they are without trying to decide whether they are good or bad. For example when dealing with a difficult situation with a dog, it is natural to feel anxious, but when we accept that we are feeling anxious, we can then control our emotions so we don't start flapping and panicking or behaving timidly towards the dog, and making the situation worse.

At face value this seems to be an easy task but it takes time and practice. This is largely due to our in-built tendency to question and seek solutions.

The following chapters will be a useful guide toward finding the answers and solutions within yourself. All that being said it is important during this time to just get used to noticing:

"When I was going through it with Kai, even before leaving the house I'd built myself up into a panic with fantasy visions of the blood and the screaming and the court case and on and on. No wonder Kai didn't feel safe going out for walk with this lunatic."

* Take notice of how you feel. Your emotions. Are you happy, anxious, upset, fearful? Ask yourself "How am I feeling?". Do this regularly throughout the day (with your reminders). Do this whenever you interact with your dog.

* If your dog is reactive outside notice how you feel just thinking about taking your dog for a walk. You will start to notice how your dog's demeanour can change depending on your mood.

* Notice your own thoughts and emotions whenever your dog's triggers are around, whether it be outside with dogs, cars, cats etc. or indoors with noises, events, other animals or even certain people.

* Is there a big difference in your dog's temperament when outside or in the house? It could be they are model dogs in the house and monsters when they go out or the other

31

way round. How do you feel in each of these situations? What's the difference?

* Observe your dog, paying particular attention to their excitement level, body language and general behaviour. Do not attribute human emotion or motive to what they are doing and you will soon start to learn what your dog is actually telling you.

* Also work on those reminders.

"As dog behaviourists we work with dogs in their own homes, so meeting a new dog for the first time causes a certain level of anxiety. We have no idea how the dog will react to us, or how much control the owner has over the dog. Although we are aware of this anxiety, we have to walk into the consultation calmly and confidently, in order to reassure the dog, and the owner. On arrival at the house, and before getting out of the car we take a few minutes to just breath, giving ourselves time to get grounded and bring our full attention to the present moment. We will then calmly and quietly meet the dog and start the consultation, all the time remaining aware of our breathing and the energy we are sharing."

The Breath Meditation

A Quick Word On Breathing for the Meditations

When we breathe normally, and especially when we are anxious or stressed our breathing tends to be high in the chest. When we are doing these exercises or meditating in general the breath should come from the diaphragm. For this the stomach needs to go in and out as we breath. If you are not used to this, place your hands over your belly button so you can feel the motion. To start, and to engage the muscles needed, push your hands out as you breath in, and pull them back as you breath out. Practice this a couple of times to get used to the feeling.

This is a great exercise to help bring you into the moment and feel a bit more grounded. It can be done anywhere and only takes a few moments.

Step 1 Stop

The first step is to just stop and take stock of what is going on in and around you. It doesn't matter if you are sitting or standing. Adopt a relaxed, yet dignified posture to tell your body and mind that you are about to do something different. Notice your weight pressing where you are in contact with the chair or the floor.

Start to notice your thoughts, feelings and any other sensations or impulses. You don't have to label or judge what you find, just be aware of it being there. Be kind, be curious.

Step 2 Breathe

When you are ready, begin to bring your attention to your breathing. To start, take three slow, deep breaths to bring your focus to it and then return to your normal breathing rhythm. See if you can focus on one whole breath in and out. When your attention is distracted, gently bring it back to watching the breath. This is what you are doing right now. Now follow another breath. Notice where the breath is most apparent for you. Notice the little gap between each out breath and the start of a new in breath.

Step 3 Moving on

Now widen your attention out to the body as a whole. Notice any areas of tension, especially around the face, jaw, neck and shoulders and gently soften these areas. Move your attention back to where you are in contact with the seat or the floor, and when you are ready slowly re-engage with the world around you and carry on.

Engagement exercise for your dog.

Getting your dog to engage with you is the first step on the journey. This is important in a number of ways. First, and most basic is, that if your dog isn't paying attention to you there's little chance of teaching even a simple command. On a more advanced level it will help you guide your dog through situations where they may not react well, as their focus will be more on you and less on the environment.

We don't encourage training with treats as a rule but they do speed up this step and can be phased out later as we don't want to become a snack dispenser. Keep in mind that treats are rewards not bribes. The treat should appear after compliance not before.

Formal training should be kept short and stimulating. Ten minute slots several times a day works best and gives you the opportunity to assess when your dog is likely to respond well to it and when he's not. If during formal training your dog starts to lose interest, cut it there. It is important to end the session on a positive so ask the dog to do something easy that you know they can do. This is termed 'formal' training because you are teaching specific behaviours, but bear in mind that every interaction with your dog has an element of training and at least one of you will be learning something. Who's teaching and who's learning?

Don't use touch as a reward during the training sessions as this can raise excitement levels. Wait until the session is finished and then give them a big fuss. This will eventually help them to recognise when training is over.

NO!

It is imperative that your dog understands the word NO, although this seems obvious and we would presume that everyone would teach their dogs this word. But, even though it is probably one of the most used words, it often becomes meaningless to the dog. For your dog to fully understand what this word means it will be necessary to show him an alternative behaviour, such as when telling him No to stop him from doing something it is important to then give him something else to do, such as 'No don't chew that' 'chew this instead' and give the dog something he can chew. No don't go there, come here instead etc. The amount of situations this word would be used are far too many to mention but it's used the same as you would use it with anyone, the difference being is that the dog will need to be told what to do instead. Also when it comes to formal training it helps to indicate to the dog when he is not doing it right and you can then repeat the command. This helps the dog so much and cuts down on the time spent on any particular training issue.

YES!

The word yes is used in our everyday communications with our dogs, often with play and excitement 'You caught the ball yes' etc and is used as an encouragement to

37

continue whatever it is that they are doing, such as when looking for the ball and he's going in the right direction we often hear yes yes that way etc. The word yes is utilised within formal training too. Whenever we are training we use simple words and phrases to communicate what we want from the dog, and yes is great for this. It's a great encouragement for the dog assuring him he is doing the right thing during the task as opposed to the praise that comes immediately after the task. This can help a restless, impatient, unsure type of dog. It goes something like this... Ask for the behaviour, e.g. "Sit". When he sits say "YES, Good Sit!". So the formula is ask for the behaviour, then say YES Good behaviour.

Release Command

Having a Release Command tells your dog that the activity is over and they are on their own time. It's a clear and unambiguous way of helping the dog understand what they are supposed to be doing at the time. Uncertainty will lead to anxiety which will lead to them making mistakes and getting frustrated. Say "Free" or "Break", or a word of your choosing, after rewarding them for completing the task.

Watch Me

"Watch me" is a really important command for your dog to learn. Eye contact is very rewarding for your dog and builds trust and a strong emotional bond. "Watch me" is also a great way to refocus your dog's attention onto you, avoiding unwanted reactivity in certain situations, or just to make sure they are ready, and listening for whatever is coming next.

With your dog in front of you, hold a tasty smelly treat in front of their nose. When the treat has their attention bring the treat up to your nose drawing the dog's gaze with it. When they make eye contact say "good" or "yes" and give the treat. To start, make it really easy for your dog by accepting the tiniest of glances, even a twitch of the eyebrows in your direction. As the dog starts to catch on and gain in confidence, gradually increase the distance between the treat and your face so they have to look further to meet your eyes. When you know that they have understood what's happening it's time to introduce the verbal cue. Eventually you should be able to hold the treat out at arms length and the dog will still be focused on you.

Then you can start increasing the time they have to hold the eye contact. Once they understand the verbal command, you can stop using the treat as a lure.

When this is starting to become second nature for your dog, start asking for eye contact in other situations like before putting their food down, before going through the door, before letting them off the lead etc. Having your dog wait and look at you in these situations builds patience, manners and self-control. Also try to notice and praise any random eye contact your dog makes with you throughout the day.

Chapter 2

Mood and Energy

So why is it important to have a calm and balanced dog? What does that look like? and how is it related to our moods and energy?

The first distinction we need to make is between 'high energy' and 'high excitement' as a lot of people think they are same. Some dogs (and people) just seem to have boundless energy. It doesn't matter how much exercise they get, how far they run or walk, they are always ready to go again. This is not the kind of energy we are referring to in this book. We are concerned with the mental or spiritual energy that can lead to high excitement and the inability for the dog to control their emotions and actions.

Probably the best analogy for what we mean by mood and energy is when you walk into a room where a couple have just had an argument and you can feel the tension in the air. "You could cut the atmosphere with a knife" is a common phrase used to describe such times. Have you noticed how quickly a bad mood can sweep through an office or any group of people? This also happens within groups of dogs where one unbalanced, frantic or over-excited dog will upset the whole group and very likely cause a fight.

Over-excitement leads to obsessive behaviours like digging or chewing, and can be the root of excessive barking, going mad at the door bell, flying at the window when someone walks past, anxiety or panic. Over-excited greeters also tend to get themselves in trouble with other dogs and can get snapped at or bitten.

There are some nuances to observe here to correctly ascertain where you and your dog are. Some dogs are just naturally full of beans and have a lot of fun and that is great, as long as they are able to control themselves and come back down when asked or required to do so.

"Kai for example, I would consider to be medium energy, high excitement. This meant two to three hours a day was enough physical exercise and she was happy to sleep in front the fire for rest of the day. Her excitement levels would however be through the roof on sight of other dogs, the door bell, familiar people etc. This often caused her to behave inappropriately as coming back down was very hard for her. In essence, she was losing her sh*t."

A lot of people we have met and worked with have mistaken excitement for happiness. You've probably heard people say "look how happy she is, she's so excited". One aim of this book is to help you see that excitement doesn't necessarily equate to being happy, but to being in an unbalanced state of mind, quite often driven by anxiety or insecurity. One phrase we use a lot is "happiness can often lead to excitement, but excitement rarely leads to happiness."

To help our dogs with this then, we need to be in a calm balanced state, and not feed in any undue excitement. We need to be monitoring their excitement levels to avoid overload, to catch it before it gets too much. A bit like when children get too excited and have to be given a time out.

Back to Mindfulness...

After going through the exercises in the last chapter (which we know you did), you may have noticed a couple of things; one is that you are becoming more aware of your thoughts, and of watching them. The other is that you may be starting to recognise that your thoughts can create the way you feel and then behave. The opposite is also true, that your behaviour can affect the way you think. For a quick practical demonstration of this, try holding a slight smile for thirty seconds and see how it lifts your mood. In fact, it's enough to simply activate the smile muscles without actually smiling. You can do this sitting at your desk and no-one needs to know.

We can then introduce the concept to you that your thoughts, that perpetual commentary running in your head, are not you (bear with us). If your brain just asked "what commentary?", that's the one. You have approximately 70,000 thoughts a day and 90% of those are the same thoughts you had yesterday and the day before that. The same thoughts lead to the same feelings and the same actions, causing you to be stuck in the same emotional rut and addicted to the way you feel, as this feels 'normal'. For examples of thoughts affecting physiological change in your body, try thinking of your favourite food and you will salivate and your tummy may even rumble. Think of something sexy and that will produce certain feelings. Think of when someone upset you or made you angry and those feelings will return.

Your thoughts are generated by your mind, not you, and your mind is yours to control.

You have a mind in the same way as you have a lung, a heart or an arm. It is part of you, but is not you. The mind is a problem solving tool that constantly looks for problems and ways to solve them in an attempt to keep you safe. You are your **Awareness** of thought, **not** the thought itself.

Ego

We usually think of someone who has big ego as being full of themselves and a bit loud, and while this can be the case, Mindfulness looks at the Ego differently.

Mindfulness views the Ego as the conscious, thinking, planning, story telling side of the mind. Eckhart Tolle describes it as our ***"mind-made self"***; the story we tell about ourselves and cling onto for all we're worth. It is the part of us that needs to be right and to make others wrong.

https://www.thepowerofnow.co.uk/

In Buddhism it is the grasping, clinging side of us that doesn't like to be made a fool of.

Richard Wilkins calls it 'The Script'. He explains this as a metaphor for the negative voice we all have in our head. He explains that if we do not **choose** how to feel, think and act, the 'Script' will make those choices for us. This is also understood as being on 'autopilot'. If you had a choice of being happy or miserable, you probably wouldn't choose to be miserable, so if you are, it's because the script is choosing, rather than you.

https://www.youtube.com/watch?v=Brj60kDsDoE

One last example would be "The Chimp Paradox" by Dr Steve Peters, in which the Ego is played out by our earlier chimp mind, getting our modern mind to do it's bidding. https://chimpmanagement.com/books-by-professor-steve-peters/the-chimp-paradox/

Fear of change

The ego fears change and differing opinions, as these represent a threat to the identity your mind has made for you. It is this threat to our view of ourselves and the defence of our long held beliefs that causes us stress and anxiety. We tend to do this mostly on autopilot. The Mindful approach to dealing with this is to notice the thoughts or feelings, stop, and simply observe what is going on in that moment. If you can, label it, *'this is anxiety'* or *'this is frustration',* but without passing judgement on whether this is a good or bad thing. Feelings such as anxiety or frustration, for example, are not comfortable and at first it is hard to just accept them for what they are. The Mindfulness exercises and meditations will help you to see and use these feelings as an object of focus. Sit with the feeling and refuse to let the mind provide fuel to the fire of those feelings. Give yourself the space you need to make a decision on how to **respond** rather than just **react** how you normally would.

Autopilot

A lot of the time we operate entirely on autopilot and this is often a good thing. Without it we wouldn't be able to drive a car, or even walk. You'd never get anywhere if you had to think about every little detail of doing either. However, we can also be on autopilot when it comes to our thoughts, feelings and actions. When something triggers us we often react with the same predictable thoughts of judgement and criticism, either towards ourselves or someone/something outside of ourselves, before we realise. Very often we never realise.

Every time something triggers a repetitive thought, that particular neural pathway gets a little stronger and eventually becomes the default thought or reaction to that trigger. This is neuroplasticity at work. Mindfulness helps us to recognise these repetitive thought patterns as they occur and gives us the opportunity to choose how to feel or react. Some examples of unhelpful autopilot thoughts would be:

- Over-generalization - "this always happens to me" … even if it's raining for everyone else too

- Disqualifying the positive – refusing to see or acknowledge anything good about the situation

- Mind reading - "They are thinking" x y or z about me, the situation or whatever

- Fortune telling - "I know what will happen if I …..."

- Catastrophising – OMG I've missed the bus. My day is ruined!!

- Personalisation – This situation is all my fault

- Blaming – This situation is someone/something else's fault

Creating Drama

As a species we seem to love creating drama. From simple embellishments to stories, to a full on arms race over who has it worst (or best), who's right, who's wrong. You only have to watch the news to see this in action.

"My drama would run something like this... I'm going to walk down the road, a dog will appear from nowhere, (despite my vigilance). Buddy will get this dog and I am probably going to get beat up, the police will come and I'll be arrested. Buddy will be taken from me and very likely euthanised. This would then justify my feelings of terror, dread, fear, anxiety. All of this before I even got my coat on. Therefore as soon as I would leave the house this story was running and my feelings would start to match it, making me physically tense and unknowingly passing all this onto Buddy. None of the above happened, but that drama literally ruined years of my walking with Buddy and to be fair to him I don't know how he coped. Lunging at the odd dog seems such a small thing when I look at it now and I wish I'd realised then that the problem first and foremost was with me, but I saw it as Buddy had a problem."

We also create an inner drama in an attempt to justify the way we feel about our thoughts, actions or inactions. When we are making big lifestyle changes like giving up smoking, moving city, a change of career or becoming the perfect dog guardians, things feel strange at first, uncomfortable, we feel 'out of sorts'. As far as the Ego is concerned we're going to make a change and this signals that we are putting ourselves in danger, straying from the known path and it doesn't like that.

Naturally the ego wants to go back to feeling safe, so will do anything it can to get us to have a cigarette or give up the diet because this feels normal, even if it is not the best for us. With practice you will start to become aware of when your ego is feeling threatened and you find yourself indulging in one of the unhelpful patterns listed above. Your mind starts to create a drama in order to justify your actions and reactions. Mindfulness helps us to notice, stop, and then choose how to respond rather than just react.

Neuroplasticity

Neuroplasticity is the brain's ability to reorganize itself by forming new neural connections throughout life.

It used to be thought that when we got to a certain age the brain was "set" or finished and it was all down hill from there. We have since discovered that this is not the case and that our brains have the ability to change and we can consciously affect that change.

Neuroplasticity allows the neurons (nerve cells) in the brain to compensate for injury and disease and to adjust their activities in response to new situations or to changes in their environment.

Neuroplasticity also comes into play when learning new skills, such as learning a musical instrument or a new language, or when making and breaking habits, such as forming a Mindfulness practice or giving up smoking.

Strong neural pathways become the default path, the usual reaction, leading to the same thoughts or actions. Using Mindfulness, we can become aware of these repetitive thought patterns and choose to think differently. And the more we do this the stronger that pathway becomes and the original thought pattern becomes less, until it is no longer a pathway.

This is the process we are taking advantage of in being Mindful with our dogs. The more that your dog gets to practice being in a peaceful state of mind the more they are going to see that as the preferred option. Neuroplasticity then gets to work and literally rewires your dog's brain for a more peaceful approach to life.

It is important to remember that our emotions were formed long ago in the evolutionary past. In fact, as soon as life was able to move independently a fight or flight response was developed. For good or bad, this is what being alive feels like.

Emotional Regulation Systems

There are three basic emotional regulation systems that work both independently and together to make up our emotional life. Mostly this is an autonomic process, but using mindfulness to help us notice and be aware of which system is activated can help us to understand where difficult feelings or emotions are coming from. We can then decide if that's how we want to feel.

The Threat/Self Protection System

The job of this system is to alert us to danger and threats to ourselves and others we care for, then fill us with feelings to help us deal with the threat. This system includes uncomfortable feelings such as anxiety, anger and disgust, that can be difficult to deal with, but keep in mind that these feelings evolved to keep us safe. The amygdala is a fast acting alert system that picks up on things that are important to us. It is the part of the brain that lights up when we perceive a threat. The stress hormone cortisol also comes into play in determining our anxiety levels and sensitivity to threats.

The Incentive/Resource Seeking System

This system's job is to guide and motivate us to seek out the pleasurable things we need to survive and prosper, providing positive feelings when we achieve this. These are things like food, sex and shelter, but it also comes into play if we win a competition, pass an exam or fall in love. When you can't sleep because you've won the lottery or met the person of your dreams, it's because this system is over stimulated. Conversely, in people with depression it is often under stimulated, making it near impossible to feel motivated. If this system gets over-stimulated and we become too 'wanting' and 'needing more', the self protection system kicks in. If it feels there is a threat to 'getting more', or the possibility of losing what we've got, this then causes feelings of anxiety and stress. The hormone involved here is our old friend dopamine.

The Soothing and Contentment System

When an animal is not having to defend itself or seek resources because it has all it needs, this system comes into play. This is contentment, or peacefulness, or being at peace. It is a different kind of happiness from the 'dopamine fuelled' seeking system. There is a link here with affection and kindness, in the way we would soothe a distressed baby, and feelings of contentment and fulfilment. Hormones are released to help calm us, and a major player is Oxytocin. This gives us the feeling of well being, like we get from feeling loved, wanted and safe with others.

It's worth mentioning here that, we should only be affectionate with our dogs when we and they are in this state of mind. This refers to the cuddles and the baby talk type of affection, not the praise and encouragement we would use when in the other two states.

Autonomic Nervous System

The Sympathetic and Parasympathetic Nervous System are part of the Autonomic Nervous System (ANS) and regulate our basic bodily functions like heart rate, breathing, digestion. The Sympathetic Nervous System is generally triggered by the fight or flight response and the Parasympathetic Nervous System comes into play to calm us down after the stressful event has passed.

Stress arouses the Sympathetic Nervous System and activates the release of adrenalin, noradrenalin and corticosteroids. This raises blood pressure, and prepares the large muscles to fight or run. The brain shuts down all non-essential circuits such as digestion, thinking and your immune system.

When we are constantly stressed our immune system gets degraded, resulting in fewer neurons being created and old neurons being overstimulated causing them to shrink. There is a decreased capacity to learn, feelings of anxiety, nervousness and low mood. We can perceive things people say and do as more threatening or negative than they are, creating even more stress.

The Parasympathetic Nervous System kicks in when the perceived danger has passed. This allows us to calm back down and recover from the stressful experience. Endorphins are released to slow the heart rate, decrease blood pressure and provide pain relief. It has been a long held belief that we have no control over the ANS, hence it was called autonomic. This has now been shown not to be the case. A very simple and obvious example of control over the ANS is the ability to hold our breath or breathe in a controlled way. We can also deliberately slow our heart rate using breathing and relaxation exercises. But it goes further. If we purposefully generate feelings of joy, peacefulness, love etc. we are literally changing our physiology and produce the hormones that enable us to be in that emotional and physical state. The science of this is called Epigenetics and is beyond the scope of this book.

It is important to realize that our emotions, state of mind and the sense of well-being are controlled by chemical and hormonal changes in the body. The chemistry of anxiety is very different from the chemistry of contentment.

Back to the dogs...

In the previous chapter you took notice of your feelings and your dog's moods and energy, but without acting on them. In this chapter you will start to take a more active part in creating a peaceful mood and energy. For example, around meal times, the front door and on walks.

It is your goal to bring your dog to a place of balance. It is not about your dog. Everything begins with your energy, your state of mind and your approach. You are the source of your dog's calm state of mind and your dog should be looking to you for guidance. If you are anxious, nervous, overexcited, angry, frustrated or even if your confidence is low, your dog will pick up on that energy, and this often leads to dogs feeling insecure as there is no proper leadership. Conversely, if you are relaxed, calm and quiet, guess what?

How Dogs Read Us

A dog's sense of smell is their most prominent sense. When they are born, their eyes and ears are closed and the only senses they have are scent and touch, needed to be able to find and feel their mother. So these senses literally keep them alive. It's not until three to four weeks later that their eyes open closely followed by their ears. It is with this incredible sense of smell that dogs interpret the world. The part of a dog's brain that is devoted to analysing scents is 40 times larger than a humans and they can identify smells between 1,000 to 10,000 times better than we can. Dogs have somewhere between 125 and 300 million scent receptors; we humans, on the other hand, have a mere 5 million.

Dogs have been trained to sniff out cancer and diabetes and can pick up on dangerous blood sugar levels even before the standard tests. Service dogs also help children who are struggling with bed wetting by waking them up when their bladder is full. This is quite remarkable.

So there is nothing mysterious or etheric about the way dogs read and respond to us; it's all based in chemistry and biology. This is why it appears that your dog is able to read your mind. The way they perk up if you even just think about going for a walk or getting their dinner can seem spooky. The real reason is that they are masters of reading body language, and they monitor you constantly. They can also detect the slightest of hormonal changes, so in situations where you feel anxious or uncomfortable, your dog will smell the adrenalin, pick up on that little tightening of the jaw. They may not be aware of what is happening, but they know how you feel about it.

So if you consider that people are bags of chemicals and hormones, and emotions are simple reactions to the release of those hormones, then it makes sense that your dog would be able to sniff these out and know what's going on. So, dogs can smell your excitement, sadness and yes, your fear!

Exercises for You

- Start to notice how much attention you give your dog, and when. Attention is anything from touching, talking to, or even watching your dog. Again we tend to do this on autopilot, so we don't even notice we're doing it most of the time. We are often sitting relaxing, then all of a sudden we'll notice that we're petting the dog or throwing a ball for them. Constantly interacting with your dog in this way can build an unnatural dependency in the dog, which may cause them to feel anxious at times when this is unavailable (for whatever reason). This can, and often does, lead to separation anxiety.

- To your dog, your attention is a major resource and a valuable reward in itself. Often this is given at the wrong times. Notice who is instigating this attention. Is it you? or your dog? Things to consider are:

  - Is he in the right state of mind to be rewarded with your attention?

  - Is he really being a "good boy", or is it more of a hopeful request on your part?

  - Are you comfortable with sharing your feelings, thoughts and emotions with your dog at the present time?

  - How demanding of attention are you? How demanding of attention is your dog?

- Affection (the cuddles and oochycoochy kind), should only be given when they are calm.

- Continue with '**The Breath Meditation**' from Chapter One. Practice bringing your attention to everyday tasks (washing up, peeling spuds etc). The more we practice, the more it becomes second nature. It's called a 'Mindfulness Practice' for a reason. It can be easy to slip into a "I'll do it later" mindset, or even forgetting to do it altogether. At first it may be a bit stop/start as you are building the habit, and that's ok, it's natural. That's why setting up reminders is really helpful.

- Introduce the **The Sounds Meditation**. Aim for 5 to 10 minutes a day. In the morning after waking, or before bed, or both is good. This exercise will start to build into a proper meditation routine. Be patient with yourself and stick with it. Sometimes it can feel a little uncomfortable or awkward at first as you may have thoughts or feelings that are unfamiliar. We don't practice to get better at meditation, we meditate to get better at life.

The Sounds Meditation

This is similar to the three step breathing exercise but takes it a bit further. First by observing your own breath and then noticing the sounds around you.

Step 1 Stop

We'll be sitting for this practice. Adopt a dignified, alert posture to tell your body and mind that you are about to do something different. Notice your weight pressing where you are in contact with the chair and your feet on the floor.

Then take note of what you are thinking, what you are feeling and any other sensations or impulses. You don't have to label or judge what you find, just be aware of it being there. Be kind, be curious.

Step 2 Breathe

Take a big breath in through your nose and let it out slowly through your mouth.

Take two more similar breaths.

Bring your attention to your normal breathing. Just watching. Try not to control your breathing. See if you can follow one whole breath in and out. When your attention is

61

distracted, gently bring it back to watching the breath. This is what you are doing right now. Now follow another breath. Notice where you feel the breath the most. In your nose? In your chest? Notice the little gap between each out breath and the start of a new in breath.

Continue observing your breathing for a couple of minutes.

If you get too distracted you can count the breaths to help you focus. Count "1" on the in breath and "2" on the out breath. Count up to 10 and start again.

When you feel ready, move your attention to the sounds around you. Don't actively listen, just let the sounds come to you. Notice sounds that are far away and then sounds that are nearer to you. Let the sounds come and go.

When your attention is taken with a thought, let it come, then let it go, and return your attention gently back to the sounds around you. Have a sense of congratulation about the process of drifting off, noticing and returning to the present moment. Be kind to yourself.

Step 3 Moving on

Now widen your attention out to your body as a whole. Notice any areas of tension, especially around the face, jaw, neck and shoulders and gently soften these areas.

Move your attention back to where you are in contact with the seat and the floor. When you are ready, slowly re-engage with the world around you and carry on.

Before walking your dog, take a moment to do the Three Step Breathing Exercise. You can do this at random times during the walk too.

Exercises for your dog

Continue with Watch Me.

Sit-stay and down-stay

What "Sit" means is, sit there until you are released. Likewise, "Down" means lie there until you are released. The stay is implied, there is no need to say it which makes life easier for your dog as they only have one clear command to process.

Have your dog close in front of you, giving eye contact, of course. Tell your dog to sit. As their bum hits the floor say "Good sit". Then release them with "Free". Throw the treat a little way away so your dog has to stand to get it. You can then repeat the exercise.

When your dog sits reliably, extend the time, by seconds at first, say "Good sit" and release.

The next stage is to take a step away backwards, then immediately step back to the dog and say "Good sit" and release. If they seem ok with that try two steps and keep building up the distance.

In the early stages work on building up duration – the time they can sit calmly – and distance – how far you go away from them. Do each as a separate task.

A useful way to organise your training is to consider the '3Ds'. Duration, Distance and Distraction. Work on each separately. When you are working on one area, take the others back to easy.

Really drill these exercises. Start by making it easy and very gradually build up the duration. Release with the Free command. Remember stay is implied so we don't need to say it. Try to notice any time your dog sits or lies down naturally and mark the behaviour with "good sit" or "good down" Keep praise calm.

Chapter 3

Body Language

Although we possess language, a reasoning mind and conscious intelligence, it is body language, (including facial expressions) that makes up 80% of what we actually communicate. Body language is something we all start to understand very early in life. I'm sure we all remember when, as a child, we would go to do something and our mum or dad would give us 'that' look that stopped us in our tracks, no words needed.

Mindfulness really helps with the whole issue of awareness around our bodies. It is in fact, our body that roots us to the present moment, as it can never be anywhere else (unlike the well travelled mind) This makes it the perfect anchor to our present.

Therefore attention to the body is attention to the present moment and it is here that we are able to learn a great deal about ourselves physically.

For instance we all have our little quirks that we will be completely unaware of, such as a head tilt to the right when doing a particular task. Now imagine doing that one little movement several times every day (unconsciously) and the effect this has on your physiology. The unnatural position of the head will affect muscles (maybe bones) in our neck, which will transfer to our shoulder and maybe down our back or arm. The point is that when we discover pain or discomfort in any of those areas, it will never be traced back to the positioning of our head as we fail to NOTICE that at all. The same can be said when operating on auto pilot while doing everyday tasks. It is helpful to ask ourselves periodically, how efficiently am I doing this, how am I standing, how relaxed are my shoulders? are my knees locked or relaxed? am I using movements/muscles unnecessarily? It is important that we start to become aware of the body as much as possible. There are many situations where being aware of our bodies can help us stay safe, for instance, when navigating a small space or having to get around obstacles. By being more aware, we can actually decide the best and calmest way to proceed without bumping into, or banging our head on something. Which, incidentally, if the bump does happen, it usually comes as a shock to us, which highlights that we failed to NOTICE our head approaching the open cupboard door or similar. There is a term for people who are often not paying attention, we call them clumsy.

The way we hold our body has a profound effect on our moods too. A common technique used by public speakers, performers and sports people is to hold a 'power pose' for a few minutes. For example, standing tall with legs apart and arms in the air. Head up and chest puffed out. Try it for yourself.

Think about the difference in demeanour of someone when they are sad, angry, happy or ecstatic. We tend to judge the mood of someone just by how they look, and a lot of this (whether we know it or not) is our recognition of their body language and the expression on their face.

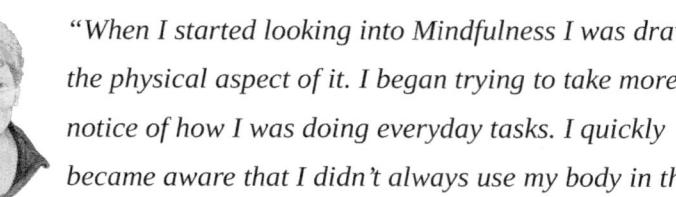

"When I started looking into Mindfulness I was drawn to the physical aspect of it. I began trying to take more notice of how I was doing everyday tasks. I quickly became aware that I didn't always use my body in the best way, putting strain and tension where it didn't need to be. An early example of this was when I was chopping vegetables and decided to focus in on how I was doing it. I quickly noticed that I was using my whole arm, right up to the shoulder to chop some cabbage. I became aware that I was using my hand, my wrist, my forearm, my

upper arm and my shoulder to do a job that only needed a hand and a wrist. I learned so much from that simple exercise and have since become much more focused on how my body moves through the world."

It has been shown that we humans show emotion on the right hand side of our faces and tests using eye tracking software showed that a dog will always look to that side first.

Excerpt from an article in The Telegraph:

Dogs can read emotion in human faces

By Richard Alleyne, Science Correspondent

6:00PM GMT 29 Oct 2008

Dogs are the only animals that can read emotion in faces much like humans, cementing their position as man's best friend, claim scientists.

Research findings suggest that, like an understanding best friend, they can see at a glance if we are happy, sad, pleased or angry.

When humans look at a new face their eyes tend to wander left, falling on the right hand side of the person's face first.

This "left gaze bias" only occurs when we encounter faces

and does not apply any other time, such as when inspecting animals or inanimate objects. A possible reason for the tendency is that the right side of the human face is better at expressing emotional state.

Researchers at the University of Lincoln have now shown that pet dogs also exhibit "left gaze bias", but only when looking at human faces. No other animal has been known to display this behaviour before.

Due to our dogs understanding of us, we are able to utilize our body language as a way of communicating with them and being understood.

When dogs communicate with each other they tend to do so quietly, (unless there is a level of excitement which encourages barking). To us a dog's body language can be subtle and very fleeting. Things like quick tongue flicks, a look away, a raised eyebrow can easily go unnoticed. There are, however, some obvious things to look out for, such as the position of ears, tail, head etc. We generally miss so much of what our dogs are saying and very often don't notice until they are barking, lunging, fleeing etc.

When communicating with your dog the language you use is just a noise, other than the few words that have a meaning attached, Blah Blah **bed**, Blah Blah **dinner**, Blah

Blah **walkies.** A more effective way of communicating with your dog is to consciously use your energy and body language rather than your voice. It really is a case of 'Silence speaks volumes'.

So find your calm, assertive stance, facial expression, tone of voice and bring your full attention to what your body language is portraying. Do you feel and look full of confidence or are you subdued for one reason or another? What are you showing your dog?

You will see how, with the right energy, you can inform and direct your dog using just your body, you can block their path, and you can move them back, creating space between you. Also just by covering an item, with your hand, such as a toy or food, your dog soon learns that he is not allowed it, and will learn to back off. You will start to notice some simple gestures that are obvious to your dog such as, turning your head or body away acts as a way of stopping demanding behaviour. All done with just your body. There is no giving commands, no shouting, or getting stressed.

"As I said in the introduction I have had dogs all my life and training was something I enjoyed and had a knack for. With Buddy I decided I

71

was going to go one step further and teach him
hand signals to every command. He took to it
immediately and I could give him commands
without the need for verbal cues. I thought I was
such a clever dick and that Buddy was one of the
smartest dogs in the world. However with my new understanding of
dogs and communication I realise that dogs don't need words once a
physical cue is understood, bringing me down to earth with a bump.
Take that EGO"

Start to become aware of your dog's body language. Notice what he looks like at particular points in the day such as when he is excited, when he's feeling insecure, nervous etc. What about when he is completely calm and relaxed, what do his ears, tail and general stance look like? The more aware you are of these signals from your dog, the easier it will be to predict certain behaviours.

Whenever we are out walking with our dogs remember it is completely different to when we are walking on our own to the shops or to work. We do need to adopt a certain attitude when dealing with our dogs or indeed any animal. It is up to us to guide them through our world.

If your dog has a 'moment', whether due to seeing another dog, advertising boards, a flapping tarpaulin, or one of many other examples. It is vital that we help them to regain their composure before moving on. If we rush the dog away from the situation there is a good chance that they will react in the same way the next time they come across it.

"We were on a walk with a client's dog, a dog who isn't particularly reactive, but on seeing a large, brightly coloured, plastic statue of a bear, she lost her mind. Her hackles raised and she immediately started barking, one of those howly "what the heck is that?" kind of barks. This was unfortunate for the people drinking coffee at the cafe where the bear was situated. Eeek! We led her away, at the same time sheepishly apologising to people with coffee all down their fronts. We walked for a while and then started the approach to the bear again. As soon as she looked ready to react, we stopped, waited calmly and quietly for her to relax and bring her attention back to us, then calmly walked away. We left the bear for that day, but on the following days we did the 'bear work' as above, getting closer every time, until she no longer reacted. We encouraged her to have a sniff of the bear, which she did. And that was the end of any issue with the big bad plastic bear."

Also by continuing our journey without addressing the issue, the dog will remain in a heightened state, so will be more easily triggered by other things in the environment. So stop, stand tall and breathe. Try doing the Three Step Breathing Exercise from Chapter One, giving your dog, and maybe yourself, chance to calm down. When he has calmed down, and if you have the opportunity, calmly return to whatever triggered him; if on the approach he starts reacting again, just stop there, calm him and approach some more. Do this until you can get much closer to it, showing him that it poses no threat.

Some basic dog body language

The following describe some basic clues to how your dog is feeling. It is important that each clue be looked at as part of a bigger picture and put together like a puzzle. The environment and situation you are in also need to be taken into account. This is all part of why we keep asking you to take notice of your dog's body language in different situations. Look back at Chapter 2 if you need a reminder.

HEAD

- A lowered head is a calming signal. This can look a lot like stalking when approaching other dogs but really they're saying "I'm OK, I don't want any trouble."
- Head turned away means "Not interested", "Leave me alone".

EARS

- **Forward** alert, defensive, curious.
- **Back and soft** when walking combined with a level head and a relaxed tail and gait - travelling mode (explained in Chapter Four).
- **Back and stiff** Could be a sign of anxiety when combined with other postures such as a stiff or tucked tail. An example of why we need to look at everything.

TAIL

- A wagging tail is not necessarily a happy dog, watch your dogs tail in different circumstances.
- **A frantic wag** is caused by excitement.
- **A slow swish** is a sign of irritation.

- A tail **held up and curved over the back** is a sign of being interested and ready for action. It is also a sign of confidence.
- A tail **stuck straight out like a stick** is showing tension in the dog.
- And last but not least, a tail that is **tucked under** is a sign of stress and anxiety.

EYES

- **Looking away** - Will look away as a calming signal and as a sign that they are not comfortable.
- **Staring at** – challenging.
- A **half moon** eye also known as whale eye is a sign that the dog is extremely uncomfortable, usually at the approach of something, it is a warning.

MOUTH

- **Yawning, lip licking** (quick flicking action) are calming signals. They are a signal to other dogs and humans to take it easy and it also helps to calm themselves. Yawning in particular is the dog trying to self calm and if done toward another dog is an attempt to calm them.
- **Frantic lip licking** indicates anxiety.

- A mouth that is slightly open with the tongue almost sticking out is a nice calm state of mind, usually goes along with "soft" eyes and ears.
- A **tightly closed mouth with stiff ears** and a stare is not good at all.

BODY

- If the body has a **forward leaning posture** it shows confidence and a tendency to not back down. A raised head and tail often accompany this.
- Conversely, a **lowered body or backward lean** is a more submissive posture often accompanied by a lowered head and tail and ears pointing back.

 *"There were a couple of dogs that Buddy and Kai really did not like. To be fair, nobody liked them. One day we encountered them coming the opposite way down the path in the park. Buddy started to make a beeline for them but Kai got in his way. Buddy tried to go around her, but again she blocked him. When he tried to pass her again she reared up, (Buddy was twice her size) put her paws on his*

shoulders and got her teeth out like she was the Alien, right in his face. Buddy stopped in his tracks and his head dropped like he'd been told off by teacher. He turned round and came back to us, letting his nemeses live another day. I'm so glad we both saw this communication between them, for it was brief, to confirm that we actually did see what just happened."

Mindfulness Activities for You

Mindful Standing (For you and your dog)

Now that you've had a few weeks of practising some of the Mindfulness exercises suggested, you should feel more comfortable and be able to attain stillness and a Mindful state for a short time. This exercise is for you to do with your dog. When starting to do this it is common for some dogs to find it quite strange and disconcerting. They may whine, bark (or both) or go round in circles. The point of the exercise is to maintain your Mindful state despite the distraction of your dog. It is just something else happening in the environment, that you are aware of, but not reacting to.

The exercise is simply to stand and be Mindful. Begin in a quiet environment with your dog on a lead, so they can't wander off. Stand for a few minutes. Don't interact with your dog regardless of their reaction, just stay aware of their behaviour by keeping them in your peripheral vision rather than catching their eye. Build up the time and the distractions gradually.

The result of doing this exercise is that your dog will be able to settle next to you, whether they are standing, sitting or lying down. Some may even doze off. This will lead on to your dog being able to wait patiently in most situations, for example, when you are out and about and you need to make a phone call or stop and chat. Once they are able to wait patiently you will be able to sit outside a cafe or pub and have a relaxing drink to reward your efforts.

Mindful Walking

Mindful walking is one of our favourite Mindful exercises. It is essentially a deliberate way of walking with your **full** attention on everything, from the ground beneath your feet, to how each foot rolls from the heel to the toe on the ground, to how the hip throws the leg forward to the movement of the upper body etc. If you can, for an added level of concentration, incorporate noticing your breath too. After practising this exercise a few times you can include your dog as well. A good way to start is to walk up and down in a defined area or do a figure-8 around two trees so there is a definite pattern to what you are doing. This prevents the exercise turning into aimless ambling. Don't forget to breathe.

Your Moves

Find a movement(s) that is easy, and that you enjoy, as a way to reconnect with your body. Have a look on YouTube for some beginner Qi Gong or Yoga videos and choose a movement you like. Do this movement(s) as many times in a day as you can. Doing this exercise is a great way of reacquainting yourself with your body and how it moves. By being aware of the body and its movements you start to notice what movements feel good and what movements don't. This then gives you the opportunity to make slight or significant adjustments in the way you do something. But remember this is not about exercise, stretching, or any other form of physical activity, it is about ATTENTION. Also continue to pay attention to your body while doing simple everyday tasks. If all that sounds like a bit of a faff, just put the radio on and have a dance.

The Body Scan

This exercise is a great way of noticing the body and its different parts. This can be done at any time of day, sitting or lying down. If done at night it is a great way to relax you for sleep or if done in the morning a great way to check on how the body is feeling and maybe the areas you need to pay attention to during the day. This exercise is again a bit more involved but is still quite easy to do. This can be a nice meditation to do to help you drift off to sleep.

Stop

You can do this sitting or lying down. If sitting, adopt a dignified, alert posture to tell your body and mind that you are about to do something different. If lying down, lie on your back with your legs uncrossed and your arms by your side. Notice your weight pressing where you are in contact with the surface that is supporting you.

Notice what you are thinking, what you are feeling and any other sensations or impulses. You don't have to label or judge what you find, just be aware of it being there. Be kind, be curious.

Breathe

Take a big breath in through your nose and let it out slowly through your mouth.

Take two more similar breaths.

When you are ready, bring your attention to your normal breathing. See if you can follow one whole breath in and out. When your attention is distracted, gently bring it back to watching the breath. This is what you are doing right now. Now follow another breath. Notice where the breath is most apparent for you. Notice the little gap between each out breath and the start of a new in breath.

Move your attention to your feet. Try to feel any sensations there may be. There may be none. That's OK. Breathe in to your feet and breathe out from your feet a couple of times.

Move your attention to your lower legs. What sense of your legs do you have? Take a couple of breaths into your lower legs.

Continue to breathe into and out of the following parts.

Bring your attention to your knees…move on to your thighs...hips...lower back...tummy...chest… fingers...arms...shoulders...neck...mouth and face...forehead...and finally the crown of your head.

Hold your attention on the crown for a few moments

Moving on

Now widen your attention out to the body as a whole. Notice any areas of tension, especially around the face, jaw, neck and shoulders and gently soften these areas. Move your attention back to where you are in contact with the seat or the floor, and when you are ready slowly re-engage with the world around you and carry on.

Exercises for your dog

The Place Command

This is a great exercise for helping your dog learn how to relax on their own and be able to wait patiently. It also keeps them from getting under your feet in the kitchen for example, or when you have visitors. The ultimate goal is for your dog to be able to go to a designated place and stay there until they are released.

This is the command that really needs putting into use as part of your daily routine, as opposed to just being a 'training exercise'.

As with most training there are many methods to achieve the same result. This is what works for us most of the time.

Choose a place you would like your dog to go to and put down a mat or blanket that is 'special' and not their usual one. This becomes their place which you can take with you to the pub or cafe or anywhere you need your dog to be able to settle.

With the dog on lead, walk to the Place and indicate for him to step on and say "Place", or "On your Place". When the dog steps on give them a treat and a "Good dog". Release them with your release command and lead them off the place. Repeat. Sometimes dogs can be a bit reluctant to step on at first but some encouragement with a tasty treat usually sorts that out. When they are comfortable stepping on and beginning to get the game, you can start to increase the duration by waiting a second or two before rewarding them, and then gradually build up the time. The next step is to add in the down or sit when they are on Place. After that, start increasing distance and distraction by walking around the Place and moving further away bit by bit.

If (when) they break the stay and get off the Place to follow you, just guide them back onto Place and reward and release. Have a little break then repeat, repeat, repeat.

When your dog understands this command it's time to teach him to 'go' to Place. You can then give him the command Place and he knows to go, without you leading him. A good way to start this is to put a treat on the Place and walk your dog away. Say "On your Place" or "Place" and let them go. Build up gradually to sending them to their Place from different rooms, or put it down the garden and send them to it. Have fun.

"When I was teaching Kai to go to her Place by the kitchen door (it's a step in our case), it went something like this. We had done the basic Place as above, so applying the same commands in different situations is easier for her. I would chop carrots, she likes carrots so its a good reward. I would take her to the step, then walk back to the counter. Of course, by the time I get back to the counter she's right behind me. Take her back to the step, go back in to the kitchen, she follows, and so on. Eventually, she stayed on her step while I got back to the carrot. I then quickly grabbed a bit of the carrot and took it to her on her step. Every time I could get back to the counter without being followed, she got a bit of carrot on her step. So now she knows if she waits, the food comes to her. That first carrot took twenty five minutes to chop. Now she just does it – whether she gets a treat or not."

Chapter 4

Fulfilling Your Dog

Dogs are in fact simple creatures and they are generally easy to please. All we need to do is put a few things in place. The first thing we need to put into place, is ourselves as the leader. We are 100% responsible for the welfare of our pets. We are in charge. So, how do we do that? First, we remove all decision making from the dog. What happens, where, when and with whom is your decision and it is the dog's job to join in when invited. We also have to, rather obviously, make sure that all of their needs are met and that they have learned to trust that we can reliably continue to meet them.

Your dog is an animal which means that they live instinctively and their goal is survival. They are in tune with nature. Like all animals, they live in the moment and communicate with energy and body language. That is why two animals of very different species can communicate and get along with each other. A dog is happiest when they are part of a pack, know their place and can work for the survival of the group.

behaviour is an outward expression of the state of mind

On a basic level your dog needs very little from you, but what he does need is fundamental to his physical and mental well being. The following are the three main areas to look at. These are the physical, mental and emotional aspects of your dog's life.

Physical

This is important because our dogs can't be expected to relax, behave or learn if they are full of pent up energy or in some pain or discomfort. Excess energy will soon lead to frustration and frustration is one of the things that leads to 'bad' behaviour. Exercise and food are two crucial factors.

Exercise

The health of a dog's joints, teeth, skin are all linked to diet and nutrition. With puppies whose joints haven't fully fused, care must be taken not to over-exercise them or let them jump from heights. Monitor older dogs for signs of arthritis and moderate their exercise to suit. Keep them at their ideal weight. Exercise needs to be appropriate for age, breed, energy levels and physical abilities. It is the quality of the exercise, rather than the quantity that makes the difference. We're generally not training athletes for a marathon (although some may be) so exercise, as with us, should be moderate. It's more about being on the move and having fun and adventure.

"Years ago I read a book by Grisha Stewart (of B.A.T Training fame) in which she was making the point that in general we over-exercise our dogs with activities that are far too physically demanding for them. She was especially negative about those ball flingers. She also said she knew she sounded like a party pooper and to be honest that is what I thought as Kai was storming around putting 150% into everything. Now Kai is older and has severe arthritis I do wonder about the wisdom in Grisha's words."

Food

Our diet is crucial to our wellness and our well-being. There are now lots of studies linking diet and nutrition to depression/anxiety in people and also the link to behaviour in dogs. Obviously food is a basic need but even this needs to be considered and monitored. You owe it to your dog to give him a good healthy diet and remain aware of the food, treats and scraps you are feeding him. Often we give dogs treats (however unhealthy) because they give us the cute face and big eyes, and also because it makes us feel good. A different way to approach this is to ask yourself "Is this good for him?" "Does he need it?" "has he done anything to earn it?" If the answer is no, then don't give it him. Food, after yourself, is your main resource and should be used wisely. The choice of food for dogs is vast and can be confusing and misleading. There is a lot of good marketing going on within the pet food industry, so don't get sucked in, do your own research and feed your dog the best your budget allows. Our personal preference based on our research and experience is to feed our dogs a raw food diet. The change to raw food was a gradual process that started with making home cooked food for our dogs. They had always had raw chicken legs and meaty bones so we knew they could tolerate the raw, but it was still a big step to go all in, as you need to be quite organised and on top of it, but the results are well worth the effort. The main motivation for home-made food was to get them off kibble and proprietary dog foods, as just doing a little bit of research on the ingredients revealed that they were not as they were portrayed. Kibble is like one of those noodle pots being compared to a balanced meal. After all, it has meat and veg and all the vitamins.

Mental

When our bodies feel good, our minds are ready to work and learn. Boredom, due to lack of mental stimulation is the quickest route to what we deem 'bad' behaviour in our dogs.

Dogs are pack animals and it is imperative to your relationship/household that your dog knows his place and what is and isn't allowed. You could call this discipline, but is in fact leadership. If you don't show your dog leadership then he will be forced to decide what is acceptable behaviour for himself, and he's just a dog in a human world so it rarely goes well. It is only fair to let your dog know that you make the rules and to teach him what they are. Always remember that dogs do not understand 'sometimes'. If he is allowed to jump up for example, then he will always jump up, even if you are wearing your Sunday best, he's got muddy paws and you are not best pleased. Therefore it is much fairer if you teach him that jumping up is not allowed, ever.

Are they mentally challenged? It's not all about physical fitness, mental fitness is just as important and a good brain workout can be as tiring as a physical one. You know how exhausted you can feel sitting at a desk using your brain all day. There are lots of ways in which to stimulate our dog's minds. These include Kongs and other food puzzle toys, training and play, and having something to do. For example going to a 'place' when the door bell rings or when you are preparing food could be considered a job for them and while they are 'on task' they can't be misbehaving.

Are there rules in place? Your rules can be somewhat arbitrary and it depends on your circumstances and what you are prepared to allow. If you don't mind your dog being on the settee, that's fine. But if they are demanding about it, or get grumpy and possessive when asked to get down, then being on the settee should not be allowed. At least until they accept that it is your settee.

"A client we saw was struggling with her rather large and bossy Akita who was becoming very pushy, very large, and hard to handle. The dog would take himself to bed in the evening, but on the client's bed. When the client went to bed a couple of hours later,

and essentially got into the dog's bed (as the dog saw it), he would get grumpy, not give her any room and get even more grumpy when asked to get off.

To desensitise the dog to being asked to get off the bed, we taught them to play the 'On/Off' game. This is done by encouraging the dog to get on the bed and then get off the bed, but only rewarding the 'off'. The 'on' is a reward in itself. The time off the bed is then gradually extended. When on and off are on cue, just don't tell them to get on. The other part of the process was to get the dog his own bed to have in the bedroom. When we went back for the review session, not only had the dog stopped trying to get on the bed, he had also taken his own bed downstairs, by himself, and that was where he now chose to sleep."

There are a few rules that should however be part of your routine and relationship. These include for example giving space around food and space around the front door which are discussed in more detail in the next chapter.

Are your rules consistent? Is everyone in the household applying the same rules? Work out between you what words and or gestures you are going to use and make sure everyone sticks to them. (Put them on the fridge next to your Mindfulness reminders.) Even down to making sure Granny isn't sneaking treats under the table.

Is there a routine? Dogs love routine. It gives them confidence and security when they know what will happen next so they can relax and behave appropriately. For example, when getting ready to go out for a walk, if you get the dog ready first, putting on collars, leads and coats, before putting your own shoes and coat on, it lets the dog know that they will be coming with you and although there can be a lot of excitement around going out, it is possible to teach the dog to wait calmly while you get ready. This leads to them leaving the house in a calmer manner which will enable them to settle into walking more easily. Your dog will soon work out that when you put your shoes and coat on to go to work or shopping, that they are not coming, without having their expectations dashed with disappointment as you close the door behind you. This can help relieve separation anxiety or stop it starting in the first place.

"On one of our behavioural consultations, we had been called in to help a woman whose dogs were marking around the house, including on the furniture. They paid

very little attention to her and she was at her wits end. As bad as this situation was, it was made worse by the fact that they were three adult greyhounds, (not the smallest of dogs, and neither are their, shall we say, deposits). We soon saw what we suspected was going on for the dogs. It was clear that no boundaries had been put in place, resulting in all three of the dogs claiming their spot on the sofa, leaving the owner perched precariously on the edge. After we explained the importance of putting in boundaries and how the lack of them negatively affects the relationship, the owner had one of those Aha moments. We advised that she immediately started setting some boundaries, starting with reclaiming her settee. She did this successfully and the dogs accepted the new order of things, without too much resistance. The marking stopped completely within a couple of weeks, the dogs started paying attention and their relationship was greatly improved. As this was one of our first consultations we were extremely relieved that she recognised and implemented what we had discussed."

Emotional

A balanced emotional life comes from feeling fulfilled mentally and physically, feeling safe, loved and wanted.

Trust is probably the most important aspect of the relationship with our dogs, even more than love. It is quite common for us to see clients whose dog's clearly love them but don't trust them, which has caused the dog to become anxious or reactive. As mentioned at the start of the chapter our dogs need to know and trust that we are going to provide for their needs everyday, all the time, without fail. Trust helps our dogs feel safe and valued. Once trust is established a more meaningful relationship can be developed. With the dogs that we foster, trust is the first thing we have to create as some of the dogs are quite discombobulated as a result of the sudden life change that has just happened to them. And it is a two way street. We also have to have to try to let them know we trust them too, so that everyone can feel safe. One of the keys to developing trust is routine. As we mentioned previously, dogs love routine. The dogs know when there will be a walk, when they will be fed, when they can relax and sleep and when its playtime. When this is in place our dogs don't have to worry or wonder if they'll get fed or walked, therefore reducing the need for them to be fretting and hassling you when they think something should be happening.

Giving Affection

Our dogs love affection from us and we love to give it, but again, as with food this is a major resource and should not be given away lightly. We cannot state strongly enough that when giving affection it is imperative that you consider your dogs state of mind at the time. If you give affection to a dog who is unbalanced, for instance, feeling anxious, fearful or over excited you are nurturing this state of mind and the dog will associate this state of mind with receiving your attention and will feel that he is being rewarded for it. It is in situations such as this where we can use Mindfulness to remain focused, emotionally neutral and physically calm, until we have helped the dog to calm down and return to a more balanced state. Now we can give praise and affection which rewards the calm behaviour. This can also help the dogs learn to deal with their anxiety and to self calm.

An anxious dog is rarely truly relaxed. They can be very needy and demanding/begging for attention. They will be constantly looking around themselves, watching and listening for any movement, maybe moving every time that you do. Part of what creates, or at least perpetuates anxiety is not feeling safe. This is as true for us as it is for our dogs, and like us they need someone to treat them with empathy, not sympathy.

Noticing the good stuff

We often don't notice when our dogs (and children) are being good and are settled and calm and they only come to our attention when they play up or start doing stuff they shouldn't. It is very beneficial if we can start to notice and reward with gentle praise when they are doing well. For example, your dog walks in the room and settles down nicely, mark it as good behaviour with a "good dog, good down", but calmly so as not to raise their excitement. Keep an eye out for, and mark any calming behaviours such as yawning, stretching or 'shaking it off'. Yawning is often considered to be a sign of stress, but it is more of a sign that they are beginning to work through it and calm down. It is also a signal to other dogs and people that they should relax also.

All of the above when taken as a whole can seem like a lot and a bit overwhelming, but you are probably doing most of it anyway. If things are not as you would like or your dog is out of sorts, you may find some of the above points are lacking, or it may be that you need to do more of what you are already doing.

Waiting

Simply learning to wait is a very important skill for your dog to learn. Waiting is a big part of every predator's day and your dog will see this as a job. You can incorporate waiting into many situations such as having your dog wait while you prepare his food and while you get yourself ready to go out etc. It is also important that on returning home from the walk he waits until you invite him in. This reaffirms to the dog that it is your domain and you control every aspect of it. Waiting can also be incorporated into games, for example ask your dog to wait while you hide some treats in another room for him to find when you release him. Learning to wait is also important for us. We may have to wait until our dog performs the right behaviour before we can reward them. Sometimes this can take a while and is a good opportunity to practice some mindfulness so that we can wait peacefully and not build frustration, which our dog would pick up on, and probably take even longer.

The Power of the Walk

Of all the things that are going to improve your relationship with your dog, and cover a lot of the physical, mental and emotional aspects mentioned above, the walk is undoubtedly the most important, and is the key to solving many other, seemingly unrelated, behavioural problems.

By walking our dogs, they not only get to stretch their legs and release some energy but this is also how they learn about their environment and feel connected to it.

Dogs are natural born travellers and explorers; stray dogs have been observed walking up to twenty miles a day in their hunt for food and fun. So when you take your dog for a walk, this is the closest thing to their true nature there is. For our dogs, this is their chance to catch up on what's going on in the neighbourhood, meet friends, hunt, play, and have adventures. We often think of the walk in terms of the physical exercise it gives the dog - and it is important to drain physical energy - but there is so much more to it than that.

The key to a successful walk starts well before you leave the house, making sure that your dog is in a calm, relaxed state of mind before you even start to put on collars and leads. *Remember that all behaviour is only an outward expression of the state of mind*, so when you reward a physical behaviour you are also rewarding the state of mind that caused that behaviour. An example of this would be when you have asked your dog to sit to put on his collar, and he did, but, he's also still bursting at the seams with excitement. When the sit is rewarded, the excited mind is rewarded also, so we need to wait until the mind has settled before we proceed. It is important that our dogs are calm and waiting patiently before we open the front door, before getting in the car, and even more importantly, before getting out of the car at the park. This all goes to building confidence, trust and communication in our dogs and gives them a sense of structure.

Dogs are natural followers and travelling is a bonding experience for members of the pack. Taking the lead on a walk is a great way of bonding with your dog by establishing and maintaining your leadership role. Again, your energy is key to telling your dog that the world is safe and there is nothing to be afraid of or guard against. If you are relaxed then your dog will be too. When you are leading, your dog has to exercise his mind and self-control to walk beside you and this too is helping to drain his energy levels. On the other hand, allowing your dog to lead and make decisions on who to meet, or where to go, or when to stop for a sniff, is stressful for them and doesn't drain their mental energy but heightens it.

Our dogs need to know that we are leading the walk as this builds trust and furthers our connection with our dogs. It is important that you recognize your dog's body language as this will signify your dog's state of mind moment by moment, giving you the opportunity to respond appropriately. This shows your dog that he can trust that you will deal with things and he can relax.

The best kind of walk is a 'structured walk'

A structured walk should include some formal heel walking, some sniffing, a bit of play and some training. Don't just let them drag you to the park, run around like a crazy for half an hour and then drag you home. You're not doing either of you any favours. A structured walk obviously covers the physical exercise, but also provides mental challenge as well. The walk is a massive training opportunity and where your dog learns to trust and follow you. Walking with your dog and providing play and socialisation also counts as affection; it's not all about hugs and kisses and treats.

The walk is a time of high excitement and is probably the most challenging time to be trying to encourage a calm state of mind. But it can be done. And it must be done. It will test the limits of your patience and sanity at times. With consistency and practice though, things improve bit by bit until one day your dog will just sit patiently waiting for you to open the door.

We have to accept that big excitement is part of it and work with it rather than against it. It's mostly a waiting game, but waiting without irritation or frustration when you have things to be doing can be tough. Do some Mindful breathing. This is a process that takes time. How much time will depend on how much practice you do and how quickly your dog picks things up. Start from where you are, accepting what it is, and go day by day. If today they are a little calmer than yesterday, or it didn't take quite so long to get out, mark that as a success.

 *"One thing I'm quite adamant about is not chasing dogs around trying to put on collars and harnesses etc to go out. I used to start the process about 20 to 30 minutes before the walk by implanting the idea that a walk was imminent. Of course this would create lots of bouncing around but it gets through that initial burst of frantic energy. Even now, ten years later, we still have to wait for Kai to pace round*

the table look out of the front and back windows to take place before
she can still herself to have her collar on. It's only a minute or two
now but that's what she has to do."

Now it's time to actually leave the house, remember that excitement levels are going to escalate when you get outside, so in the early days it can be like starting the process again. But this all goes towards what we call 'generalising a behaviour', ie, transferring what they've learnt in one situation into another. Specific training around the door and loose lead walking training will need to be done independently of the walk.

It can be tough at first waiting for the dog to relax and can cut into your walk time. Don't worry too much about this, as the dog's mind is being worked and that can tire them out almost as much as physical activity. It doesn't take them long to work out that being calm and polite is what gets things done and pretty soon it will just be normal.

"Don't take your dog for a walk; go for a walk with your dog!"

Have him next to you on the lead, and just walk. Initially, he doesn't decide where to go, what to sniff, or where and when to pee. If your dog tries to drag you towards a scent, turn him away and when he has relaxed you can either lead him back to the scent or if he's taking his time to become calm, carry on walking then encourage him to have a sniff about when he is calm. This way you are letting the dog know that you say where he goes and when. The sniff then becomes a reward. If they signal they need to toilet properly, not just mark a spot, and you are in an appropriate place, then obviously you should allow them to do so. Please remember to pick up after your dog.

Dogs have a certain way of moving when they are 'in the zone' you could say, and is referred to as 'travelling mode'. It indicates that your dog is calm, relaxed and happy to just walk with you. When your dog is in 'travelling mode', they move fluidly, they are light on their paws, their ears relax back and they are focused on just walking. It is important that your dog spends time in travelling mode when you are out together. When you have walked a while and your dog is more relaxed, encourage them to start using their nose and have a good sniff around to get all of that day's news. Here you can use a signal like "Go sniff" or use your release command to free them from the obligation of walking to heel and to communicate clearly to them that they are now on their own time. This is another great way of draining their mental energy. If it is possible, and your dog is calm, let them off the lead for this activity. If your dog likes to play with a ball or run around with their friends, walk with him first making sure he spends some time in 'travelling mode', then let him have that play. By starting the game when the dog is calm it will be easier to bring his excitement back down when the game is over. Afterwards put him back on lead and get him into travelling mode again. You can do this as many times as you want for as long as you want. Having your dog on and off lead at different times on the walk will reduce anxiety around the lead representing home time and the end of the fun. Whenever you are planning to make the journey home, whether on foot or by car, make sure your dog is in travelling mode first, ensuring the excitement and energy levels are right down.

Taking your dog for a walk and providing play and socialisation also counts as affection; it's not all about hugs, kisses and treats.

Final thought

As part of a structured day incorporate special 'cuddle time', 'play time', 'training time' etc. If your dog is over-demanding they soon learn that they will not miss out on anything, they just have to wait.

There's a saying that goes something like "A tired dog is a good dog", but I don't think that's quite right because the dog can have rest and then the opportunity for mischief increases. It would be more correct to say "A *fulfilled* dog is a happy dog", as they will be more content as a way of being, not just when they're knackered.

Mindfulness Activities for You

Continue to notice how you feel in different situations, making the Mindful decision to choose the peaceful option.

You have a few options now to help you get into that Mindful Place.
  • The Breath Meditation
  • The Sounds Meditation
  • Mindful standing
  • Mindful walking
  • The body scan

Remembering to do them is the biggest hurdle so refresh your reminders to try to keep this top of mind throughout the day.

Exercises for you and your dog

- **Wait** – Earlier in the chapter we talked about waiting and it's many applications. It is easy to incorporate into your daily routine activities. Please note that as long as your dog is waiting calmly it doesn't matter if they sit or stand on their head, as long as they are calm. If you ask them to sit they are now in a sit/stay and no longer in wait. The Wait as a command means pause what you are doing and wait for what comes next. This is something neither of us actually did formally, the dogs just picked it up from repeated use. Use it before putting their food down. Waiting at the roadside. Getting out of the car. It's great in games such as hide the treat, or waiting before they can chase the ball.

- Continue with previous exercises.

It may seem like a lot to take in and remember at this stage, but keep at it and it will soon become part of your routine with your dog. It's a bit like when you are learning a new skill, for example learning to drive. At first it's a lot to remember and takes a lot of thought to co-ordinate the actions, but with practice it soon becomes second nature.

Chapter 5

Etiquette

Etiquette can be thought of in terms of manners and respect, we expect this from other people so why not our dogs? It also helps to establish ways of behaviour in different situations. Be aware that however you let your dog treat you, he will treat other people and very often other dogs. This has the potential to cause you embarrassment and get him into trouble with people and dogs alike.

If your dog is allowed to excitedly jump up and climb all over you in the house, he will naturally assume that his behaviour is acceptable, and that any person is fair game. This is not always appreciated by family, friends or even the workman you may have in your home.

Now imagine being in the park and your dog approaching other dogs with the same gusto he has learned from his human interactions. It is the energy of the dog he is approaching that will determine how the meeting goes. Some dogs will be fine if they are of a similar energy, but approach a dog who is balanced and respectful and your dog will be told that his behaviour is unacceptable. This could be by chasing him away, growling, barking, baring of teeth or pinning down. None of these behaviours are meant to harm your dog, he is just being chastised, that said, some dogs can be more forceful than others. If the other dog is not so balanced, a situation like this could easily turn into a fight.

These are the key areas to consider.

Indoors

EVERYTHING in the house is yours, not theirs. From the moment your dog comes into your home they need to know their position within the household. This starts by inviting them in and confining them to certain areas of the house, decided by you, it's your house and where they go is up to you. They need to understand that everything is provided by you from the roof over their head to the food they eat and toys they play with. This is why it is a mistake to leave food down for dogs as it takes away the fact that you have provided it, the same with toys. A hard chew toy should always be available to your dog but other toys are better given by you. It is important that you teach your dog to give up toys/food when you ask for it. They need to understand that we can give and we can take away at any time. Once this is established it makes it much easier for the dog to understand that whatever he needs/wants will be provided by you. So when he sees a tasty looking shoe/slipper he will know that it belongs to you, and if he was allowed to have it, you would give it to him.

Personal Space

This is the most important thing to have in place and will prevent many other unpleasant or pushy attention seeking behaviours. All of us have a bubble around us and if someone stands too close, uninvited, we start to feel very uncomfortable. It is important that your dog gives you this space, as you would expect from another person. Obviously when we want a cuddle with our dog we 'invite' him into that bubble, but it's not cool having a dog jump on the sofa, walk all over you or sit on your head when you are trying to relax, read or do some knitting etc. Personal space is also important to your dog and we should award them the same courtesy. You'll start to notice when your dog doesn't want interaction and that should be respected. Put their bed in a place that's out of the general flow of traffic, where they can rest undisturbed, and make it a rule not to bother them when they are on it.

Space around food

A dog with respect for personal space will understand and respect your wish for space much easier when you are dealing with food. If a dog is not used to giving space, then preparing food can be a bit of a nightmare. It can be especially annoying and even dangerous to have a dog getting under your feet, crying, begging and in some cases stealing food if the opportunity arises. Also if your dog is close to you and you drop something it will be a natural reaction of the dogs to pick it up and eat it. By making them give space it is easy to prevent this happening, and after all you don't want your dog thinking that if it's not in your hand it is no longer yours, Everything is yours! This is where Place command is useful in giving them a place to go to in the kitchen, or just outside, to keep them out of the way while still being able to see what's going on.

The closer your dog is to the object of their desire, be that food, the door, a person or another dog the harder it will be for them to exercise self control. Distance is your friend and the further away they are the easier it will be for them, and you.

The Front Door

An open front door and access to the outside world is very exciting for your dog and getting out of the door is very rewarding for them. Your dog must have permission to cross this threshold, both in and out. Whether they go through first is not as important as waiting for permission and entering or exiting calmly. This reduces anxiety around the door, fearing your dog may bolt. Or when visitors arrive it can be nerve-racking having to let someone in and stop a dog from getting out. It is also quite rude of a dog to welcome guests without permission and before you do. This can lead to a dog believing that he is making the decision to allow people/dogs in. This becomes a problem if, for whatever reason, he decides that he doesn't want that person/dog in on this day, at this time, in that coat, the list is endless and probably unfathomable to us as humans.

Leaving Your Dog at Home

Leaving the house should be done as calmly and quietly as possible so your dog starts to associate your absence with being calm and just chilling out until you return. Don't make a big fuss of leaving and promising you won't be long, just leave. Of course, if we have to go out for some time we would have taken the dog for a good walk first.

Before you go, giving them a chew toy filled with food, such as a Kong, will give them something stimulating to do. Then they are more likely able to sleep until you return. Remember it's none of your dog's business when you go out. Sounds a bit harsh, but it's easier on your dog.

Returning Home to Your Dog

Your return should be a very calm time and ideally your dog would greet you with a sniff and a wagging tail. In return you would respond with a gentle stroke or pat on the head, being aware of your energy and ensuring that there is no excitement. If your dog is overly excited on your return, wait until they calm before greeting them, this can be hard but worth it. We are not ignoring the dog, just not interacting with them, until they are in the right state of mind.

Doorways and Stairs

Imagine approaching a doorway and your husband, wife, son or a stranger barged past you to get through the door first. This would be considered rude and disrespectful and would not be tolerated. So why would we tolerate it from our dogs. Also imagine if your dog learns that it is ok to race through the door ahead of you. Imagine that there's been an accident and there is glass all over the back yard, that could potentially be very dangerous. When out walking in the countryside would you really want your dog running through gates ahead of you when you have no idea what is beyond that gate. Another big concern is the amount of dogs that get lost each year from bolting out of the front door or the garden gate.

If you've ever had a dog clatter into you from behind as they try to get down the stairs before you, you'll know how dangerous and painful it can be. Have the dog wait for you, (another training opportunity to instil patience), or give them permission to go first.

Outside

Meeting and greeting

When you are introducing your dog to new dogs and people, they should be calm and relaxed and so should the dog or person he is greeting. It goes without saying that you also need to be calm and relaxed, as you are the biggest influence on your dog's behaviour. A good way to introduce dogs is to walk them together. You can start at a distance walking parallel to each other and gradually get closer, or have the more uncomfortable dog follow behind and slowly catch up. This is another opportunity to take notice of your dog's body language and determine whether he is comfortable about the meeting. To ignore your dogs communication could lead to squabbles between the dogs and maybe an argument between fellow dog walkers.

When out walking with your dog, if you feel on edge approaching other dogs, stay calm and relaxed and envision passing with no problems. A good tactic is to smile and find something you like about the other dog. Give the dogs some distance, by walking in an arc around the dogs, which is how they behave naturally. This gives the dogs plenty of space and prevents any unwanted confrontations. Say hello to the person you are passing as this helps to relax you, your dog, the other person and their dog or dogs.

Off Lead Dogs

This applies to dogs on extendable leads as well. Do not let your off lead dog approach a dog on a lead as dogs on leads automatically feel more vulnerable as they are trapped. How the meeting goes will depend a lot on the other persons reaction and therefore the energy they are sharing with their dog. Just because your dog is friendly doesn't mean the meeting will go well, as the variables are many and unpredictable.

If you are approached by an off lead dog and are not comfortable, breathe, relax, put your dog behind you and use your body and energy to block the other dog. Keep an eye on your own dog's body language and signals.

Fights

If your dog is involved in a squabble or a fight, stay calm and get the dogs under control first. Do not get drawn into arguments with owners; just walk away if they are aggressive. If they seem reasonable ask them if they or their dog are injured and check your dog. If your dog has injured another dog you need to offer to pay the vets bill. Walking the dogs together after a squabble is the best thing to do if possible, as it will calm them down and prevent them becoming enemies.

 *"Once upon a time there was a dog who was a little unpredictable around other dogs. Kai was at a stage where she could play with dogs that were of a similar energy and liked to play rough. We met one such dog at the local park. She was, in some respects crazier than Kai but without the reactive tendencies. Whenever they met, they would charge around like a couple of maniacs until they would both collapse in a happy heap. Then one day, for reasons unknown, a fight*

broke out between them. The other dog got bitten and Kai's ear was torn right down the middle. The owner, again for reasons unknown, became very angry and aggressive and gave me a right load of abuse and then stormed off in a rage, dragging his dog behind him. The dogs were never friends again.

Conversely, a lot of the friends we have made, both dog and human, have been because our dogs had a fight. I believe this is because in each of these cases no-one got upset or angry, everyone was apologetic and put most of the blame on their own dog. I've had some amusing 'one-upmanship' type conversations about who has the biggest idiot. I understand that some people get upset and angry, and even embarrassed, which hurts their ego and they lash out to protect themselves. Seeing the other dog and owner as kindred spirits, who are probably having a similar experience as you, helps in so many ways."

Dogs and the Law

If your dog does approach other people it is important that he knows how to behave; for example, if he jumps up someone and they feel afraid they are within their rights legally to make a complaint about your dog. This can lead to you being taken to court and your dog deemed dangerously out of control. If this happens it could lead to you being issued with a DCO (dog control order) This means that your dog will have to be kept on a lead at all times.

We can see that if we want our dogs to be respectful and well mannered, we need to have earned that respect and set out our expectations of what good manners are. This is built up when we are fulfilling their needs (Chapter 4) and providing calm and consistent leadership. This has all stemmed from just a slight change in the energy we approach our dogs with (Chapter 2). When we come with presence and awareness and an unflappable calm it completely changes the way our dogs feel about us and dramatically improves our relationship with them.

Mindfulness for You

How are you progressing with the Mindfulness exercises we have suggested? We've looked at a few now, so you may have more idea of which ones you like and which ones you are not so comfortable with. You may, at this stage be feeling like "I've tried but I just can't stop my mind from wandering". Remember that's part of the process. You will never stop your mind, that's not possible, so simply be aware that you are now following your mind and gently return your attention back to your point of focus.

When meditating you may find that there is a settling in period as you wrest control from your mind and wait for it to settle down. We're not very used to just being still and not thinking, so it does feel unusual. Take your time, start to find your way, notice how it feels for you, each time will be different. Is it the same thoughts that come up each time or a constant to do list? Just notice.

Try to make a regular time for meditation. A good time is just after you wake up, before thoughts of the day start to intrude. Doing one of the exercises before bed is also beneficial. I challenge you to get to the end of a body scan while lying in bed without falling into a deep sleep.

Pick your favourite exercise and stick with that for a week and see if you can increase the time of the practice.

- The three breath exercise
- The sounds meditation
- The walking meditation
- The body scan
- Standing with your dog

Guided Meditations can be helpful at the start of your Meditation journey as they help you maintain focus. This is especially useful with the body scan and longer meditations where it is easy to get lost. To accompany this book there are audio versions of the above meditations that can be downloaded for free from our website.

"When starting out on my Meditation journey, my first thoughts were, 'how hard can it be?' Just sitting still and doing nothing. Well, let me tell you how it actually went for me the first time I decided I was going to Meditate. I switched off all devices, lit a candle, burnt some incense, sat quietly, relaxed with a straight spine, all the things I'd heard were necessary to Meditation. I'd also heard that the breath is key, so I sat with the intention of just watching my breath (again how hard can it be?). In, out, in, out, in... yet... unbeknown to me, my mind had decided to use this quiet time to consider things that, I should be doing, things I haven't done, things I want to do, conversations I may have ... and then I remembered that I was supposed to be watching my breath. I tried just focusing on the breath a few more times, but with the same result, I eventually gave up in a huff, thinking this Meditation lark just wasn't for me. This was a few years ago now, but with my new understanding, I know this is a common experience for most new Meditators, it's natural. Mindfulness has taught me that thoughts will come, but the secret is to give them no attention, see them and let them go. More recently I tried doing a body scan and it went something like this , lying in bed I directed my focus,

to the top of my head, moving on to my forehead, eyes, cheeks, jaw, neck, only to wake up 8 hours later. This was when I decided to try a guided audio version and that really helped. But even using this at first the body scan would go something like this. I would be following along lovely, head, forehead, eyes... then.... how did we get to knees? and where has my attention been? I wasn't aware of any thoughts I was attending to, but they were there in the background. Mindfulness has changed this for me, that said I still often fall asleep before the end of the body scan, when I do it at night."

Practice with your dog everyday

- **Leave** – A command that covers everything from your shoes and handbags, to squirrels and tasty treats they may find on the pavement.
  - There are a couple of ways of teaching this. The 'standard' dog training class way is to hold a tasty treat in your fist and let the dog try to snuffle it out. When they stop and move their nose away, open your hand and let them have the treat. Repeat this until they start to associate moving away with getting the treat. At this point

introduce the verbal "Leave" command and then praise with "Good leave" and give a different treat – not the one you've just asked them to leave. This method is fine if your dog has a soft mouth and is not too enthusiastic about getting the treat.

○ For the dogs that don't yet understand gentle or you don't want your hands that close to their mouth try this. Have your dog on the lead in front of you and show them the treat. Ask them to "Leave". Throw the treat a little way off and prevent the dog from going for it with a little pop on the collar and reiterate "Leave". Do this with three treats and then walk the dog away a few paces and reward them with different treats than you've just asked them to leave. Repeat this a few times. (Your next challenge is to pick up the treats you've thrown without your dog getting them first.) When they are getting the idea you can start to generalise the command to different objects.

• **Door manners** – This applies to the front door, or any door that leads to the outside world. Ultimately this is about permission to cross that threshold. You should be able to open the front door without your dog bolting out. Just as importantly it sets the tone for the rest of the walk by having you in charge and your dog paying attention to you.

- The success of this training is mostly down to persistence rather than any special skill or technique. It's good to practice this when you're not actually going out, when you can be a little more patient. Or you could incorporate your practice into the beginning and end of the walk. To be honest though, as long as you're really consistent, it only takes a few days for the dogs to get it.
- As we mentioned, distance from the desired object is your friend.
- When you and your dog are ready, with collar and lead on, have him sit as far away from the door as possible, while still being able to hold the lead. If your dog is super twitchy, putting them in a Down can reduce the trigger to move.
- Give the "Wait" command.
- Open the door. Do this as you normally would. Avoid the instinct to slowly creep the door open

in anticipation of your dog making a bee-line for it.

- If your dog does make a move for the door, simply close the door, take the dog back to where they were and start again.
- If they don't immediately move, reward with "Good Wait", and then release them to follow you through the door. Following you out is the ideal, but we realise some front door areas can be quite tight for space, with limited room for manoeuvrer so it is OK to let the dog go before you, so you can close the door for example. As we said, it's about permission to cross the threshold.
- When you've managed to get outside, reverse the process to come back in. Remember that permission is also needed to enter the house as well as leave it.
- Timing is important. Don't wait for your dog to fail. If they initially wait for one or two seconds, and that's an achievement for them, take it as a success and get your reward in quickly.

"On a pack walk with the behaviourist", there was a "Did I just see that?" moment, that was later confirmed by Jackie. Kai had by this time become one of the teachers in the pack, helping new dogs learn the ropes. Sometimes a little too enthusiastically. Anyway, on this occasion, a young dog had joined the pack and apart from being over-excited, he hadn't yet got the idea of respectful greetings or giving space. I saw Kai sidle up to the side of him and lean into him. She then slowly pushed him out of the pack and into the hedge bordering the field. She just walked off, smiling, leaving the other dog tangled in the thicket. This was probably his first proper lesson in manners. He was always respectful to Kai after that."

Chapter 6

A Review

Congratulate yourselves folks…

You now have a mindful approach to dog ownership.

(you have gone 'Beyond Obedience')

Welcome to the world of leaders and followers. It is now time to step into the role of true leadership with your head up and shoulders back, showing your dog they are safe because they are with you, and you are making the decisions.

Throughout this book we have shown how nurturing a calm and peaceful state of mind, within yourself and your dog, naturally puts you in the leadership role for your canine companions. We also highlighted the need to approach dog behaviour in terms of *state of mind, energy and fulfilment.*

Ensuring that your dog's *physical, mental* and *emotional* needs are consistently met, creates a stable, balanced energy. This leads to a calm, peaceful state of mind, and state of mind is the precursor to all behaviour.

A Review

Chapter 1 introduced you to Mindfulness, what it is, and how to start your Mindfulness journey. We talked about taking notice of your thoughts and emotions when interacting with your dog and also being aware of your dog's triggers. This is probably the most important chapter of the book, as everything leads on from there. We looked at the difference between formal and real world Mindfulness and the ways in which it is beneficial for us and our dogs. Your formal Mindfulness practice started with the Three Step Breathing exercise. Try to do this as often as you can, maybe using the reminders we talked about. We looked at how Mindfulness can be introduced into daily activities and how setting those reminders can help you develop the Mindfulness habit.

In chapter 2 we looked at mood and energy and how this affects your dog's state of mind and therefore his behaviour. We discussed how you need to be the source of your dog's calm state of mind, and the need to find this within yourself first. We looked at the ego and it's role in creating drama and went a bit deeper into the science behind Mindfulness and how it works physiologically. We introduced the Breath and Sound Meditation which expands on the previous exercise and shows that anything can become an object of focus for your meditation. We encouraged you to start *deliberately* noticing certain aspects of the interactions between you and your dog.

Chapter 3 looked at body language and what it means when interacting with dogs. Dogs are masters at reading your mood, just by your body language and hormonal cues. Bearing this in mind, your body language needs to match what you are saying. This encourages us to develop strategies such as Mindfulness in order to focus on our body.

As our dogs cannot communicate with us through language, it is imperative that we learn to recognise their body language. Doing this helps us to really get to know our dogs and indicates to us how they are feeling moment by moment. It gives us the opportunity to provide guidance and security for our dogs in all situations, especially where they may feel uncomfortable. This helps us to understand what our dogs need from us in that moment. The more you watch your dog, the more you notice things about them and can discover sides to them that you hadn't seen before. And it is great fun!!! We introduced the first Mindful exercises for you to do with your dog, which were Mindful Standing and Mindful Walking.

Chapter 4 discussed the fulfilment of our dogs in terms of their physical, mental and emotional needs. All of which have to be met if we are going to have a happy, well balanced dog.

We placed great emphasis on the importance of a structured walk. *Mastering the walk* will have the biggest and most positive effect on your relationship and your dog's behaviour.

We looked at the importance of teaching your dog to wait and gave examples of where this has proved to be useful. (everywhere)

Chapter five was about etiquette (manners and respect). It is something we expect from other people and should expect it from our dogs too. We discussed the importance of personal space for ourselves and our dogs. We talked about understanding that however your dog is allowed to treat you, he will treat others. It is important to take into consideration how other people are likely to react to the behaviours of your dog. We touched on some fundamental behaviours that need consideration such as, space around food, indoor meeting and greeting and doorways. We looked at outside, when meeting and greeting, and the importance of your dog getting this right in the face of other dogs and people. It is your responsibility to ensure that your dog understands exactly what is expected of him. We also touched on the law regarding the behaviour of your dog.

We suggested choosing your favourite Mindfulness exercise and focusing on that for a while. Try doing it with your dog.

Everyday training

We have frequently talked about formal training and given you a few exercises to help your dog (and you) learn some self control and patience. As important as this kind of training is, you must also be aware that training of some sort is happening every time you interact with your dog. Simply put, you are either encouraging or discouraging a behaviour. With every situation and interaction one of you is learning something. Be mindful of who is doing the teaching.

Know your dog and what fulfils them: this is what distinguishes a good owner from the rest. They are honest. They are real. They accept. They are in touch. They are present. They are respectful. They are balanced and they know their dog. By setting some simple boundaries and a few rules you nurture a healthy state of mind and create a peaceful, balanced relationship with your dog.

We would now encourage you to go back to the beginning. Back to being mindful, being aware and just taking notice. But this time notice how you are aware of different things than you were at the start of the book and of how your relationship with your dog has changed. Try to make these things part of your routine and way of life with your dog.

It all starts with state of mind, energy and fulfilment

Printed in Great Britain
by Amazon

17964495R00079